WITHDRAWN
UTSA LIBRARIES

D1015541

DRIVING DIGITAL

DRIVING
DIGITAL

MICROSOFT AND ITS CUSTOMERS

SPEAK ABOUT THRIVING IN

THE E-BUSINESS ERA

ROBERT L. McDOWELL,
Vice President, Microsoft Corporation

AND WILLIAM L. SIMON

HarperBusiness
An Imprint of HarperCollinsPublishers

HarperCollins books may be purchased for educational, business, or sales promotional use.
For information please write: Special Markets Department,
HarperCollins Publishers Inc., 10 East 53rd Street, New York, NY 10022.

FIRST EDITION

Designed by Debbie Glasserman
Printed on acid-free paper

Library of Congress Cataloging-in-Publication Data
McDowell, Robert L., 1945–
    Driving digital : Microsoft and its customers speak about thriving in the e-business era /
by Robert L. McDowell and William L. Simon.—1st ed.
        p.   cm.
    ISBN 0-06-662092-9
    1. Information technology—Management.   I. Simon, William L., 1940–   II. Title.

HD30.2 .M395 2001
658'.05—dc21   00-047288

01   02   03   04   05   /QW/   10   9   8   7   6   5   4   3   2   1

To Lissa, and my parents, Larry and Dorothy,
and to Arynne, Victoria, and Sheldon

In three years, every product my company makes
will be obsolete. The only question is whether we'll
make them obsolete or somebody else will.

Bill Gates

There is probably no company today for which the same is not true.

By now, every businessperson who doesn't live in a sheltered cave feels the force of change blowing, not just a gale wind but a hurricane, disrupting all we thought we knew about how to survive in a competitive environment. Every organization on the face of the globe, it seems, either has an Internet presence already or is in the midst of creating one.

But throwing up a Web site doesn't automatically qualify an organization as being ready to "do e-business."

E-business isn't just about a new channel for sales and marketing; e-business is about entirely new ways of running any business.

When Bob McDowell spoke to me about this book, he said he wanted to share some ideas on how companies could successfully adapt to the e-business era—not the tactics, the technical nitty-gritty, but by developing new visions and strategies demanded by this rapidly changing business climate.

Bob has been gathering the experiences for this book through his eleven years at Microsoft. But that was only the beginning. He has been a point man for the company, spending less time in Redmond than out talking to chairmen, CEOs, technology leaders, and other senior executives throughout the U.S. and in Europe, Asia, Australia, and elsewhere.

To a large extent, the book that has resulted gives voice to many of those forward-thinking executives, who shared their stories of challenge, struggle, battles lost and won, as they transformed their organizations to survive the storm of business changes.

In these pages, Bob and coauthor Bill Simon pull together the best ideas for taking the next critical steps that will impel your own organization forward toward survival and success in the digital e-business age.

Enjoy the journey.

—Steve Ballmer

The problem is never how to get new,
innovative thoughts into your mind,
but how to get old ones out.

—DEE HOCK,
creator of Visa,
as quoted by Price Pritchett

Technologically Illiterate
Managers Should Quit *Now*

In mid-1996, *The Wall Street Journal* ran an article chuckling over the way corporate CEOs were resisting computers for their personal use. The mocking headline read, "Computer Illiterates Still Roam Executive Suites."

Among the executives coming under sharp-eyed scrutiny was General Electric's chief executive Jack Welch, a man renowned as perhaps the best corporate leader in history. But, according to the article, Welch "didn't have a personal computer in his office until several months ago," and he "has yet to find time to try it." As for understanding the Internet, Welch had owned up to backwardness, calling himself "a Neanderthal."

By 1999, though only a year away from his publicly announced retirement, Welch decided that leading GE into the new technology era couldn't wait until his successor took over. Now describing the Internet as "the most revolutionary thing to happen since the Industrial Revolution" and "the most exciting thing I've seen in business" (this from a man who had been running GE for nineteen years),

Welch launched a company-wide effort under a banner labeled "DestroyYourBusiness.com."

A flood of speeches, memos, and e-mails carried the same blunt message to the GE business managers: change your business model, or somebody else will. As one company manager described this sudden shift, "If you want to keep working at the company, you definitely embrace the idea. It's not optional."

Reporters began to claim GE employees had taken to calling Welch "e-Jack." As they say, there's no zealot like a convert.

Still, Welch worried whether the company had the needed kinds of employees: "Do we have the right gene pool; do people who join big companies want to break glass?" And he didn't delude himself it was going to be easy: "We've got to break this company to do this—there's no discussion, we've just got to break it."

Clearly Welch had become convinced there's a sea of change going on in corporate America. Some managers and company leaders have already shared his conversion . . . some haven't but only need a little convincing . . . some never will. Companies led by those who don't understand the changes being brought by the Digital Revolution, who don't grasp that IT—Information Technology—needs to be seen as a strategic weapon, won't be with us very long.

If that sounds dire, if it sounds like something that nobody but a Microsoft executive would say, just remember: throughout the history of American business, size and profitability had been no guarantees of longevity. Of the hundred largest U.S. companies at the beginning of the last century, only sixteen are still in business. Nearly half the companies on the *Fortune 500* list in 1980 were gone from the list by 1990. Nearly *half* had disappeared from the top!

It's striking when a company in an industry widely looked on as hidebound, traditionalist, and about as adapted to change as a dinosaur, confounds expectations.

Early in the year 2000—appropriately timed, as if to usher in the new century—Ford Motor Company chairman William Ford and his CEO Jacques Nasser took turns at the podium in front of a crowded press conference to announce a new program. Their company would provide a free personal computer to each of its 350,000 workers, from the executive suite to the production-line workers and the cleanup crews. *Everybody.*

Free.

Not for use at work, but for their homes.

And not just a computer but a modem and printer as well, plus Internet access at the bargain price of $5 a month.

Why? The incredibly generous offer wasn't motivated by good-natured hearts or pure generosity, but by an understanding that a company must have a technologically literate workforce to remain competitive in today's world, and that an Internet-savvy workforce is an essential part of making this happening.

Nasser called the move part of the company's strategy for staying on top of fast-moving electronic business developments as it strives to be consumer driven.

"It's a competitive advantage for us," he said, pointing out that many of the employees would achieve a new level of capability. At the same time, he saw the move as bringing technology to "people who have been outside the fence of opportunity . . . so they can participate in this golden age of wealth creation."

The following day, Delta Airlines became the next major U.S. corporation to make a similar offer—subsidized personal computers and Web access to all employees.

It's too early to know whether these deals will prove to be empty and expensive grandstanding or a major step into the future. But one thing is clear: The leadership of Ford and Delta were each taking a major leap toward remaking their companies for the age of e-business and the Digital Revolution.

You have to admit it's quite a shift for corporate top management to think this way about the requirements for remaining competitive. What is it that makes this era so much different from the past?

. . .

The era of computers in business that began in the 1950s and '60s, in what we now refer to as the mainframe era, depended on those Cadillac-sized machines that could only be operated and made useful by highly trained specialists in white jackets, looking something like a mob of heart surgeons gathered for an operation. And although the early mainframes packed no more computing power than the machine now sitting on your desktop, they were soon producing near-miracles. Even if Trans World Airlines could have hired enough people to run a worldwide reservations system, how would they possibly have coordinated all the paperwork on a timely basis to know which flights still had seats available, and to know, when you turned up at the counter, whether you really had a confirmed reservation? No major airline would have been able to find enough humans on earth to make a paper-based reservations system work.

Then along came the minicomputer. The concept here, eventually called "distributed computing," aimed at bringing the horsepower closer to the user and so bestowing greater flexibility. Finance needed different kinds of record keeping and reports than Manufacturing, and Human Resources (still called "Personnel" back then) had different needs than Sales. Each could now store their data and have their reports structured to their particular requirements, a generous improvement over the standardized stuff that came off the mainframes. A triumph for specialized needs.

Next, of course, came the microcomputer, initially sneaking in the back door one at a time. This time the case wasn't made for the organizational impact; the case was made for empowering the individual. It was heralded in part by a flood of studies on how personal computers would empower the typists of the earth: "We can take any typists, measure their typing speed, and guarantee that word processing software will increase their output by at least 50 percent." So the promise went—a promise of boosted productivity for the individual. (Meanwhile we began to hear a lot of talk about "the paperless office," which was meant to describe a glorious future but sounded to me about as valuable as a paperless bathroom.)

VisiCalc, the first PC spreadsheet program, let people crunch numbers more quickly than with a slide rule. Eventually there were database programs, graphics programs, and all the rest.

What were these progressive stages really but the evolution of computing a little closer to the end user. Did it change the core of the business? No. A company still did payroll, still did purchasing, still did marketing, but now presumably did these things more efficiently, with greater productivity. What we celebrated as progress was focused on the plumbing—the mechanics of how you did the computing. No small achievement . . . but none of it changed the strategy of how the business was being conducted. It didn't change how you thought about your business, decided on your next generation of products, or marketed your goods and services.

But when this little whirlwind called the Internet hit us, it launched what we'll call the macrocomputing era. The central notion this time is not about the plumbing—not about the mechanics of computing, or the technology, or even the benefits issues like productivity.

My main contention that underlies the whole of this book—in fact, the belief underlying the motivation for writing it—is that the changes in technology are remaking the world of business, radically changing the way business needs to be done.

What system a company installed in the past to do purchasing or finance or Human Resources wasn't a life or death issue. Today the new era of technology is changing things as fundamental as the strategy of a company, its basic organizational structure, the very nature of the way it does business. The Internet changes everything from operating details to how managers and executives function. And there is not an organization—public or private, government or nonprofit—for which this isn't true.

It also changes the role of corporate leadership so drastically that I have been telling high-level audiences, "If you're a CEO or business-unit manager in any organization, in any industry, any-where, and you're technologically illiterate, you have a moral obli-gation either to catch up *now* . . . or to quit."

The first time I said that to an audience of business executives, I began to hear a rising noise level of shuffling feet. A lot of people in the room figured I was talking straight to them. And they were right.

I'm not arguing you need to go back to college, or hire a high school technogeek to sit at your elbow and interpret technobabble for you. I am arguing, though, that you need to learn a new way of thinking. The Freightliner story serves as a case in point.

Several U.S. companies manufacture the big-rig trucks, those up to 18-wheeler behemoths that roll along the interstates day and night, moving our groceries and toiletries and clothing and office supplies. Some years ago one of these truck makers, Freightliner, hit some bumpy roads, and in 1989 hired a new CEO, Jim Hebe (pro-nounced "HEE-bee"), to fix things up.

Hebe sent the company management team out to do some home-work, and what they reported back stunned him. He told me later, "Here we were, the biggest manufacturer of trucks in the United States, and we discovered that the people who buy our products don't think of themselves as buyers of trucks. Their business is mov-ing stuff. This thing called a truck, for our customers it's just another something you can load stuff onto at one end of the line and unload it from the other.

"This industry for years focused on increasing quality and reduc-ing costs. And Freightliner had done a pretty good job of that. You know, when I'm honest about it, so had our competitors. But it turns out what our buyers mostly care about is being able to move product twenty-four hours a day, seven days a week. They simply want a platform that will keep on rolling."

So Hebe has this apocryphal vision: "It isn't trucks, guys, it's this other thing, this 'keep 'em rollin.' " And what he tells his people is,

"We need to focus on differentiating ourselves from the perspective of the customer."

Okay, that's not an earth-shattering revelation. It's what happened next that's the crux of the story. Hebe is a classic truck manufacturing guy; he's not a PC lover at all. But he recognized that the solution he pictured had to have a technology base. Because what he figured was, "If a truck pulls into Peoria with a brake problem, it just sits there until we can get the part delivered that the mechanic needs. So if we can manage the parts inventory better, we can get that truck back on the road quicker."

Hebe talked to Freightliner's Information Services manager, Rob Hassell, and Hassell was sure they could find an available software product that could handle the parts inventory problem. They did; as soon as it was up and running, Hebe sent the sales force off to pitch the distributors on the proposition that selling Freightliner trucks would produce happier customers because Freightliner could guarantee arrival of parts sooner, which would mean less downtime for the trucks.

And that worked so well, the Freightliner people figured, "Let's take it a step further. What can we do to catch a problem before it's even become a problem?" Rather than just waiting for a truck to come in to be repaired, they started looking for a way to have constant diagnostic monitoring that would link seamlessly into Freightliner's parts system. So the company would be collecting diagnostic information on a truck while it was still moving. When the system detects that something is wearing out, mechanics are alerted and the repair can be done even before the part breaks down.

All in all, Freightliner was able to bring a dramatic improvement in uptime for their trucks, which translated into steadily growing sales.

Moral? Companies need to stop buying technology as technology, and instead approach technology from the other direction: once a business need has been identified, define the problem, and then buy technology to solve the problem.

To me, what makes this story both extraordinary and telling is that Jim Hebe came to Freightliner with long experience in truck manufacturing and no more competence or experience in technology than any other typical corporate leader. Which is to say, very little. Not an advocate for technology, not a flag-waver for computers, but just a manager who saw a business need and recognized that technology might hold a solution.

Along the way, Jim Hebe took one other step that showed he was learning the new lessons of doing business in the digital age. On the organization chart at Freightliner, as at so many other companies, MIS had always been a box under the Finance Department. MIS manager Rob Hassell had fought the good fight, but without success. As Hebe saw the impact that technology was having on the company's bottom line, he began to understand that technology input ought to be part of all important business decisions.

Today Rob Hassell carries the title of chief information officer. He reports directly to CEO Hebe, has equal status with the other top executives, and serves as a member of the Executive Committee, the company's chief strategy, policy, and decision-making group. The attitude is, If we're talking about strategic planning, we need to have somebody that we respect as a peer, who constantly provides a sanity check on the technical realities and alerts the other managers to new opportunities offered by the latest technological wonder.

Still, the transformation hasn't been entirely without difficulties.

Rob Hassell:

> Late in 1999, I reported at an ExCom meeting about a group I had put together with a goal of strategizing on e-business and e-commerce. Jim asked for input from the other ExCom members and was greeted by silence. Nobody else had even begun to think about e-business. He got ticked off, and asked for the once-unthinkable: He told me, "Find a book that says what's going on, and I'll have everybody read it over the holidays." I picked out Unleashing the Killer App, *because it was a book about technology but talked in business terms, not technical terms.*

Hassell reports that when the group gathered for its January meeting, people looked scared. They had understood the message of the book: If you don't get involved and start using these technologies, your company will be passed by. But the shock therapy had worked. "Our people now look at how we need to reinvent ourselves, and how technology can help do that," Hassell says.

It plays in the other direction, as well: The company's technology people now frequently act in the role of business consultants, at times even, on their own, suggesting solutions to business problems.

New attitudes about technology aren't the only reason, but the company's market share has risen from 16 percent in 1988, to 25 percent in 1995, to 37 percent in 1999—making Freightliner the market leader in its industry.

While most companies haven't yet heard the clarion call about what the Digital Revolution truly means, some are absolutely backward on the subject. An executive of a leading international firm confessed in an e-mail to us that his company "is one of the more cautious when it comes to security and safety. There's a concern by some in the corporation that corporate-owned PCs in the home create a potential liability since an improperly installed or positioned PC might fall on or otherwise injure a person." Incredible. But apparently not confined to just that one company: "There are those in many corporations who argue the pros and cons of this view in conferences I attend," this executive says.

Encourage workers to use technology more effectively? Not at this company. "There is the concern that if we gave PCs to employees, we would be viewed as expecting them to do overtime work for free." And there's more: "We believe in fair pay for fair work, and we do not want to get into arguments or lawsuits because of misinterpretation. We do have the policy that a manager can authorize a home machine if one is needed for business purposes." Great . . . until you hear the caveat: "The machine is to be used only for

business purposes, and the employee signs a form to that effect."
Ouch.

In large part Freightliner's new success began when Jim Hebe figured out he couldn't continue thinking about technology separately
from the business but had to find ways of integrating technology
into the planning process.

What keeps other managers and leaders from reaching a similar
conclusion and getting started with remaking their business for the
Digital Age? All the usual suspects—politics, stupidity, bureaucracy,
turf battles, and inertia.

Dangerous stuff. The question is no longer "if." People who are
still delaying face a serious problem. Managers and executives who
haven't begun thinking that way are going to get caught looking
backward and wondering, What did we do wrong?

Sure, lots of business managers will read that and think, We
know the problem, but upper management only talks about it and
never does anything. Or, Why is he telling us this, we've heard it all
before. If you're already a believer, if your organization is already
embracing the changes—congratulations. But many managers who
read this warning will choose to ignore it.

Yet the issue is survival. There will be organizations in the near
term that will shrivel and get blown away because they were willing
to believe the message that the world was changing, but failed to
accept how radical the change would be or how fast it would come.

GE's Jack Welch has his own view of that landmark of the Digital Age, the Internet. He calls it "number one, two, three, and four"
on his list of priorities. In the process of sending GE spinning off in
a new direction, Welch has set the pattern for involvement by the
CEO and managers.

Today the e-conomy and the Internet have changed the whole
equation, with the Internet proving to be more than just a new
channel for gaining access to customers. It also represents a shift

that will change nearly every company's business model—including business models that have driven some industries since they were started.

That's why I keep drumming on this idea that "if you're technologically illiterate, you have a moral obligation either to catch up *now* . . . or to quit."

What steps do you need to take to "catch up now"? For every organization, that's the key question at the dawn of this new century. Read on.

CHAPTER 2

Technology is the delivery mechanism that enables e-business, but ultimately it's the personal, it's the interaction of the human beings one with the other, that makes the company either highly successful or only run of the mill.

—Ed McDonald, Texaco

Taking Technology in Hand

The manager of any organization, in any industry anywhere, has to be intimately engaged as a user of technology during this revolution. That's the catalyst for changing an organization's business model, whether you're a governor reaching out to citizens, or a Jack Welch at General Electric trying to figure out how all your businesses can take advantage of the Internet to compete.

The CEO of a prominent company came up to speak with me after a talk I gave at a conference some time ago. He wanted me to know how much he agreed with my views about communicating, and assured me that he himself was a dedicated e-mail user. "At the end of every day," he said, "I have my secretary print out all my e-mails so I can take them with me to read at home."

Now there's a man who just doesn't get it.

Microsoft is certainly one of the leading examples of a company where e-mail is central to the culture. Any employee would have to be just plain stupid to announce, "I'm not going to use e-mail," or even, "I print my e-mails out and take them home with me every night to read." They would put themselves totally out of the loop, because everything you need to know about what's going on in the company, in your department, even in your own work group, gets passed by e-mail. It must be years since I've received any interoffice memo on paper. *Years.*

Want to raise an issue with your department head at Microsoft? Send her an e-mail. Want to know what your local manager sees as the business prospects at the end of the quarter? Send him an e-mail. Want to know what Bill Gates and Steve Ballmer have in mind as new priorities for the company? Read your e-mail. At Microsoft, without e-mail, you'd be as cut off as if you'd gone to live on a desert island.

For a large company . . . for a company that's spread out . . . for a company that has distant vendors and customers . . . for nearly *any* company in today's global economy—e-mail is as essential for staying on top of business as the telephone. Maybe more so.

Sure, virtually every company uses e-mail today. But how universally? How pervasively?

What's the predominant form of communicating in your own organization? What's the preferred form when you want to communicate with a senior executive—a vice president, the CFO, or the CEO himself? The question lingers: How come some companies get this, and others don't?

It's a truism to say that in just about everything of importance to a company, the CEO has to set the pattern. That's Business 101. And if a business-unit manager isn't using e-mail for communicating, you can bet many people in her department aren't, either. If the CEO isn't, many people in the company won't. If *you* don't, many of your people won't.

But if you show that's the main way you're going to communicate, everyone in your organization will soon follow suit. Or find themselves left out.

I have a particular reverence for leaders who see the future and lead the charge—especially when they're leading people who need to be convinced or didn't know they were ready to follow. One example that sticks out in my mind happened in, of all places, Costa Rica.

The population of Costa Rica is roughly 3.5 million—about the same as Los Angeles. It's a stable country, and the government for some years has been dedicated to improving the education and health care of the people. In the past, historically, its major export was bananas; today it has an Intel plant and its major export is computer chips.

The man who took office as president in 1998, Miguel Ángel Rodríguez Echeverría, is a wonderful person—dynamic, highly articulate, and with the best qualities of a leader. He was eager for the government to be an example to the population about the importance of using technology and being literate in technology—and found one risky but clever way to show it.

As a representative of Microsoft I was in Costa Rica in April 1999, when the government was inaugurating its new messaging system. There was to be television coverage of the occasion, and President Rodríguez decided he would go on the air using the system, to set the example: If people saw him using a computer to communicate, he figured that the populace was more likely to try it themselves. And he wanted me to appear with him. He speaks good English, I speak little Spanish; it wasn't clear what my role was going to be, but of course I agreed.

Which is how I came to be appearing on live television out of San Juan, Costa Rica. The red light on the camera had hardly blinked on before President Rodríguez turned to me and said, "Bob, we're going to send a message to Bill. What's Bill's e-mail address?"

He types in the address as I recite it for him, and then this sixty-something-year-old man starts writing his message to Bill Gates. He's no polished typist, and he's sitting there hunt-and-pecking, composing his message. He types some, he makes mistakes and has to back up and correct them. He asks, "What else shall we say?"

Finally, one letter at a time, with this national television audience watching, he gets it done. He runs the spelling checker and corrects some mistakes, and sends it off.

When we were off the air I said to him, "You go out, you're in front of everybody, no rehearsal, you futz around, you make mistakes with the camera right on you. What a class act!"

He said, "That's exactly what I wanted to do. I wanted them to see the president of the country use this himself, and make some mistakes; it doesn't blow up, and you don't feel bad about it, you just get on with it."

The humility in appearing before a live television audience and having to ask for Bill's address, asking for suggestions of what to write, making mistakes, using a spelling checker, correcting some words he had misspelled. I still think of that as one of the greatest instances of leadership by example I've ever encountered.

At the other extreme: The CEO of one of the largest U.S. pharmaceutical companies recently told me the story of an old-time buddy of his, who is on his top management team.

This man said to the CEO something like, "Look, I've got three years to go. I don't think I have to get with this program. I'll just keep operating the way I have been." The CEO reported that he thought to himself, "Maybe he could make it through those three years but I'm not going to let him ride it out—it'd be a disservice to the whole company." What he said to the executive was, "Fine— you'll never hear from me again."

A drastic position to take—especially with an old friend. But it worked: The guy went back to his office, called Information Technology to have a computer installed, and learned how to use it.

Use it how?

When we talk about becoming "computer literate," what does

that really mean? More specifically, what does it mean for a manager or executive? What is the knowledge pool and skill set you need to master, to qualify as competent for carrying the banner and leading the way for your people to become effective soldiers in the Digital Revolution?

Okay—ask a dozen experts and you'll get a dozen different answers. (Which of course is true about almost anything you ask the experts; some—extraordinary to me—even proclaim that e-business will prove a fizzle and the Internet itself will become a hollow shell, a playground for hobbyists, hackers, and the lonely. But then, there were some who didn't think the Industrial Revolution would amount to anything, either.)

Anyway, here's my own personal view on the subject: To be able to understand this powerful new tool that opens the door to these new ways of doing business, you need to be a user of technology at a reasonably competent level.

You should be able to look at spreadsheets and know the commands for moving around to different parts and different pages of a large financial document. You should know how to examine the assumptions that the calculations are based on. And you should be able to amend the spreadsheets, or at least add your comments.

Even if a secretary or some staff person handles your schedule, you should be able to use your personal calendar—able at least to do the scheduling yourself when the person you ordinarily rely on is out ill, on vacation, or otherwise away from your beck and call.

You should be using e-mail (using it yourself—not having your messages printed out for you to read at night). Everybody's nine-year-old is already doing this—has probably been doing it for two or three years, at least. As far as I'm concerned, any manager or executive who doesn't know how to handle his own e-mail should be embarrassed enough to get up to speed before the end of this week.

You should be able to read messages, forward them, save ones you will want to refer to later (or know how to copy and paste into a word processing file), send messages with attached files, and save incoming attachments to an appropriate location or folder on your computer.

E-mail is now evolving into something more elaborate; the favorite label to describe this enhanced version is "messaging." This adds, for example, "collaborative" software: rather than me just sending you a plan for your comment, you and I and several others can share in creating the plan. Producing the financial report for the closing of the quarter can involve all the relevant people in a collaborative, e-mail-based process in which all can access the document and make comments, or, depending on their level of authority, even make changes. Multiple authors, working on the document simultaneously.

And all of that, too, as soon as available in your organization, should become a part of your skill set—things you can do readily, painlessly, and without having to ask for help.

One other requirement that appears on my list of essential abilities: You must be an active user of the Internet.

By "active user," I mean you should routinely be doing the following things, at least:

Visiting your own company's Web site, becoming familiar enough with it that you are sensitive to the experience the-average-man-in-the-street has when first arriving at the site. Is the site attractive, appealing, well designed? Colorful? Does it use animation effectively to grab attention, but avoid the animation overload that makes pages slow to load and visually annoying to visitors? Is the design appropriate to the kind of prospects and customers you're trying to attract—business customers versus consumers, for example?

Is the site so well organized that it's easy for a visitor to find what she's looking for? Are you gathering data from visitors that can be used in marketing, and that can guide product managers in tailoring goods that meet what the customers say they want? And so on. You have experts designing your advertising, yet you have no reluctance about speaking up when an ad campaign doesn't meet your expectations or isn't working, based on a level of discernment you've formed for evaluating what constitutes a good ad in your industry. You need to develop that same degree of discernment about your Web site. Especially since the Internet, a few years from now, just might be the most powerful channel for marketing, finding new customers, and moving your merchandise—possibly the most powerful channel since the beginning of commerce.

Visiting the sites of your main competitors, becoming familiar enough with them that you understand the subtleties of each company's e-business approach and how it differs from yours.

Getting important pieces of information readily, on your own. Your company's stock price, breaking news of significance to your industry, the prices of raw materials crucial to your business (chromium in Kazakhstan, nickel in New Caledonia, or whatever) . . . all those key data points that you know you need to run the business, keep your customers happy, and stay in front of the competition.

Each manager and executive will have a very different list, but regardless of your position and authority, it will contain those tidbits of data and news that you should not be waiting for some underling to bring to your attention a day late, a week late, or never. You now have the ability to stay instantly abreast of the make-or-break information. If you're not doing that already, it's easy to learn how and to have a "digital dashboard" tailored to make available at a single click all the data you most often want. This is do-or-die, folks. If your competitors are already up to speed with this and you're not . . .

In the e-business age, even some of the most fundamental of a company's processes need to change. One aspect of this was highlighted in our conversation with Janet Dang, founder of the Revenue Optimization Council and CEO of greenowl, a company that does business performance consulting. At the time of our interview, Janet was general manager of applications for an Internet company called Brio

Technology. She has specialized in developing packaged business applications in the areas of decision-support and decision-making applications, and "analytic" applications that automate processes.

This focus gives her an outlook on corporate processes from a distinctive vantage point. In her view, most companies today are still a long way from being ready to do business on the Web.

Janet Dang:

> Companies that have very informal marketing and selling processes have to make these processes much more formal, and they have to think about how to translate them into technology—for example, the rules for how to handle different segments of the company's customer population in a way that's effective for each of those segments.
>
> Selling and marketing today are done by really talented people who know intuitively how to do it but who don't do it in a formal way. And that means companies are facing a fundamental change in business processes because, for the Internet, the business process has to be embedded in technology. And it's not just marketing and selling but other parts of the business as well, such as purchasing—you could have a whole supply chain process driven by technology.
>
> Sales and marketing are an art more than a science today and that's a huge part of what you're going to put on the Web. Yet even within my own company, if I talk to the sales force, they say, "We're selling to the Fortune 100." If I go to marketing, they'll tell me, "We're marketing to Fortune 2000." Do you think those are the same models? Of course not. And then if you go to the working levels and ask the same questions, it's even more different—which is scary. But every business that I go into is like that.
>
> A company like Sun will say, "We target our top fifty customers." But they can't tell you what they should be doing with each of those top fifty customers to maximize their revenue from them. And if they don't agree on how you serve those top fifty, they can't build a Web site, because they don't know what they're trying to accomplish and how they're trying to accomplish it.
>
> The companies that figure that out and figure out how to translate the right method onto their Web site will be winners. They will have much more

effective ways of working with their partners over the Web—purchasing, sell-ing, and so on—because it's really about the process.

This is one of the places where people make huge mistakes. I'm working really closely with this, and I'm disappointed in how companies are using the Web. It's a great opportunity for them and it's just hard to get them to see how to use it.

An example of a company that's ahead of the pack? Janet quickly names one that leads in many other areas as well.

Cisco understands how their Web site fits with their business model. And they're augmenting their existing business model with their Web site. They've already been thinking about who's coming to their site and what are they trying to accomplish and how do you make those things possible.

They know this is going to change their business incrementally, so they're starting out with a little piece of their integrated business.

That really is a business strategy *approach—they know that they're not just selling online. What they're really doing is giving purchase information online, and it's information that would be very difficult for them to give in other ways. It's a range of their professional expertise that they've captured and put on the Web.*

Because Microsoft is a technology company, we're obviously more directly impacted by changes in the technology landscape than companies in the real estate industry, pharmaceuticals, steelmaking, or the like.

So it's small wonder that Microsoft offers a prime example of how nimble a company must be in this Digital Age, to avoid being steamrollered by change. The story of how we transformed the company for the Internet is a case in point. Familiar in broad out-line, it's a fascinating case history.

Many midsized and large companies like Microsoft use complex financial software packages provided by one of several major companies in this very specialized field. These packages have to be tailored to the needs of each customer company, to meet the unique requirements of their industry and the way that particular company is organized and operates. The process can take months or years until the complete package is tailored and installed, company people have been trained, and the switchover is complete. As you might guess, the software is not inexpensive; price tags in many millions of dollars are common. And, of course, it needs to be upgraded regularly, adding a recurring cost on top of the initial expenditure.

Companies are already beginning to tell major software developers whose products they use, We don't want to buy your software anymore, we don't want to keep upgrading it; instead we want to *rent* it. We'll pay for our people being able to access the software. But we always want to be using the latest version, so we won't be paying separately for upgrades anymore. Oh, and, by the way, we want the software put on the Internet; that's where our people will access it when they want to use it.

You may recognize this as the application service provider, or ASP, approach, which by 1998 was already a $900 million business that would, according to the GartnerGroup, grow to $23 billion by 2003. What I think was the catalyst for Microsoft to begin taking this approach seriously was the growing awareness in the software industry that the pattern was going to shift from a packaged-product sale to a service sale. Steve Ballmer, now our CEO, picked up on the idea and began to get people in the company thinking and talking about it.

We started batting this topic around in about 1998. Our vision statement used to talk about a PC on every desk; now we're talking about a world where some device can connect with another device, anywhere, at any time.

At the time of the Windows 95 launch, Federal Express told us we were its biggest customer on the West Coast. That's because the product came out in millions and millions and millions of copies, most in a separate, shrink-wrapped cardboard box. And what we're basically anticipating for the future is that applications like Word or Excel may instead be products you'll subscribe to as a service.

Here again the Web is the catalyst. The first impact of the Internet was giving people a new ability to communicate. Then it became a marketing vehicle. And then it became a new channel of distribution. Once the impact of the Web became clear, the next questions were, Why do I have to own all the software that I need for doing payroll, and word processing, and so on? If the Web really is this network that touches everybody, why can't I use it to get access to those services? It's this thinking that led to the notion that Oops, maybe you don't sell software anymore, maybe you just need to make it available for use over the Web. Why does the user care about owning it?

Under this way of doing business, the software company doesn't collect a sales price or license fee up front anymore, but they have instead a very healthy stream of service payments, which go on forever or until the customer or company decides it isn't satisfied and wants to switch to a competitor's software instead. The buyers choose the level of service they want to pay for; the sellers no longer have the expense of a new round of product sales every time the next major software upgrade is released.

But wait a minute—Microsoft is also in the software business, and your company is liable to come to us some day soon and say the same thing: We don't want to buy your products anymore, we want to rent them. And every home user of our products—the games as well as the spreadsheets and word-processing programs, the server software, and the rest—is liable to make the same demand.

Microsoft and other developers will probably find that we need to balance our offerings—providing in-the-box software for those who want it, and Internet-based, pay-as-you-go service for those customers who prefer that approach instead.

All of this, I expect, is good for the customers, who can then opt for this new approach and select just those features they need. And good for the developers, because we get not just that ongoing revenue stream, but a stronger connection to the customer. Companies already offering software this way are finding that it brings a different kind of relationship, a *service* relationship that creates a longer-term connection and a closer level of intimacy. Another step forward in thinking of customers as partners.

How likely is this scenario? It's already happening. Are we concerned about it? Yes, very—it means an entirely new business model, with lots of uncertainties. Like nearly every other company in this industry, we have virtually no experience or history for understanding what this would really mean, how it would actually work, how we would shape a business model. And how on earth would we price it? A lot of questions—and this paradigm just might be full force upon us before we have the answers.

But we're also highly excited about the prospect of offering software as a service, which seems to represent a great opportunity. We'll still have to work as hard at upgrading the software to keep ahead of the competition, but we won't have to keep going out and convincing all our customers why they need to upgrade to the newest version.

My point in all this: It's another powerful illustration that thinking about new technology used to be the province of a company's technology wrangler, the IT boss; the CEO had no reason to be involved in which payroll system the company would use, or which word processor.

But technology issues today, increasingly, are in the category of issues that demand the highest-level attention.

Executive leadership. As we've already acknowledged, it's almost a cliché that the person at the top has to show the way.

Managers and executives need to set the example for using technology to do business in the new e-business/Digital Revolution style. But—a notion we'll return to frequently in these pages—what we're talking about here is a whole new way of looking at and using technology: not technology per se, but technology as a means of achieving a goal.

A prime example of this can be found in how the city of Charlotte, North Carolina, has tackled its challenges. As cities and states seek to differentiate themselves in the quest to attract new plants and new corporate offices, Charlotte has found a successful formula less obvious than tax breaks and matching funds, in a movement instigated through the leadership of the city's fortyish mayor, Patrick McCrory.

One of the early efforts in this direction was bringing in a technology director who could pump some energy into the thinking. The man they chose, Guy Cavallo, came from the business side but had also had public sector experience.

Here's how Mayor McCrory and Guy Cavallo tell the story—

McCrory:

Atlanta has been the queen of the new South, but we thought Charlotte could start challenging and become an example of a rapidly growing and progressive city.

Out of this initiative we've become the number two financial center in the country. With the success of that, I think it helped lead the city to say, We also want to have a showcase city organization just to keep up with the success of the financial industry here.

Mayor McCrory understood that this would mean upgrading the technology infrastructure. Once the effort got under way, the city went out looking for someone who could lead the operation. When Guy Cavallo was contacted, he spent some time in Charlotte looking over the situation, and saw that the city's technology lagged years behind.

Cavallo:

Before I accepted the job, I asked for a full citywide network diagram so I could see what type of infrastructure they had. I also asked about the type of infrastructure they wanted; the answer was that they wanted something which would connect all city workers and departments together in a single system.

What I saw instead was a city that had been wired with cable television wires. I had to tell them their existing infrastructure would not support the new systems that they had already bought and were in the process of implementing. We would have to rebuild the entire infrastructure—from the wiring to the data.

The mayor had to shift gears and gain City Council support for moving their technology in a new direction. Key question: How does any organization gain support for technology purchases?

McCrory:

I believe technology needs to be a political sell and not a technology sell.

That's "political" in a broad sense—with application not just in the arena of government, but in the arena of corporate politics, as well.

Cavallo:

If you try to obtain funding for any major technology project based on the technology alone, in most cases you will fail.

My predecessors tried to sell the rebuilding as a series of separate components—a wiring component, a router/wide-area-network component, a desktop component, and a software purchasing component. They thought this would be an easier sell because the funding would be spread out.

I saw that as a liability because it's hard to show success based on the implementation of any single component. No visible success generally means no more funding, so I put it all into one package and said, "It's all or nothing, you've got to do all of these things together." That also helped protect the funding because they couldn't pick and choose individual pieces. Most importantly, we put as much into marketing all of these changes as we put into designing the technology.

I see a lot of my peers not understanding this strategy. They'll go out and try to convince business line managers that they should invest in additional network bandwidth, or eight-way servers, or other types of technology without tying it into the bottom line by telling their internal customers, "Here's the impact on your business."

What you need to do is prove to business managers or department managers that their business is going to be better off by using the technology. And if you can't explain to them in business terms why they'll be better off, you shouldn't be offering it to them.

I'm not talking about making traditional return-on-investment business cases. I'm talking about explaining commonsense business reasons. Technology is moving so fast in so many areas that you usually won't have the luxury to do an ROI before making decisions like whether you should invest more on your organization's Web site. It may mean the difference in your company's survival, so is waiting for an ROI analysis worth it?

McCrory:

We were redoing the technology structure of the whole city government. Naturally there's a fear initially on the part of employees—Gosh, this automation is going to eliminate my job, or, Am I going to be turned into a keypunch person and not a professional . . . and so on.

Guy and his people went out of their way in terms of how they implemented it. He got my endorsement, he got the support of the City Council, they set up training resource centers where employees in a very nonthreatening way could come and get comfortable with the new hardware, new software. They really saw it as an opportunity to sell to the employees that what they were doing here was investing in them.

Cavallo:

People are often resistant to change and we know that. That's why a key part of our effort was providing one-on-one help to every employee in the city as they migrated from old technology to new. We developed a multiple-tiered transition strategy that included low-cost classroom training through the city's training center, citywide demonstrations with Q&A sessions, com-

puter-based training at every desktop, and transition manuals to help ease
the migration to the new Exchange e-mail system.

We also placed full-time professional trainers in every department until
their migrations were completed. This allowed all of the staff members to
receive immediate help with any problems they encountered on their own
computers. Throughout the project I consistently received very positive feed-
back about these trainers.

McCrory:

They wanted the city employees to see the new technology as a better way to
serve the citizen, not as a secret way to cut 20 percent of the staff. Whether
they're in private sector or public, all change is painful for people. Why
should they change to let you put in different technology, even if it's better
technology? You need to show them that they'll be better off.

This aggressive commitment to making people feel comfortable and edu-
cated to be able to use it, I believe, is one of the things they did really wisely.

Charlotte has what amounts to fourteen different business operations that are all set up to run independently as one entity. In the
past, those separate businesses hadn't been able to agree on any
common technology schemes, not even on the same network systems. We all know about department heads and business-unit managers who run their own fiefdoms with fierce independence. Guy
found a deucedly clever way of dealing with one staunch holdout.

Cavallo:

One department head—I'll call him head of the "Yellow District'—had been
hard to convince of the benefits of cooperative projects from the centralized
IT department. This is a guy who has spent his entire career in the Yellow Dis-
trict and has advanced all the way through the ranks. With that lifetime of
service, he has come to own the Yellow District. And he will tell you that—it is
his district! And in fact, the Yellow District was collecting enough in fees to
cover his budget, so he didn't need to look for funding the same way the
other city departments did.

This man absolutely hates anything from city management. When I went out to meet with him, he sat me down in his office and told me point-blank, "You're from uptown, I don't want anything from uptown, I don't know why you're here, but don't waste my time."

He had his own technology staff—three full-time people plus some part-time. So we built a relationship with those staff people. We showed them our designs for the infrastructure and desktop configuration, and won their support for implementing the standard systems we had developed.

But they retained control of the systems, which made it a win-win situation for everyone. They even got to take full credit for the project with the Yellow District director.

So the Yellow District now has systems that run the citywide standards.

As with just about everything in life, good communication is fundamental. The Charlotte people have recognized that poor communication with the workforce has been a common pitfall for technology.

Cavallo:

There are so many rumors with technology projects, and people always seem to twist things around. So the first thing you have to do is show that you care about their day-to-day productivity and that you're not just there to roll out the next version of software products or servers regardless of whether they need them or not. I established a number of committees that meet on a monthly basis to make sure that we're always communicating our plans and that staff know where we're headed.

McCrory:

The city manager has a regular meeting that every supervisor in the city attends. Two or three times a year, Guy gives that group an overview of what's coming in the next six months. And then he answers the questions and concerns that individual people have.

Cavallo:

We put several groups together. One we call an IT Investment Review Team, a group of about eight top managers of the city, who review all citywide technology standards and spending. We also have an IT Advisory Group that includes either the business manager or the technology manager, or both, from each one of the lines of business operations. I don't chair this group because I don't want people to think it is an IT-owned-and-run operation. I'm just one of the participants.

We also put together a technology forum, open to anybody who wants to meet once a month on technology. I make sure that all of the senior managers from my network operations, information systems, Help Desk, and quality-assurance operations are there. It's designed as a free-for-all, answering any questions and addressing any rumors.

If we're going to make changes to the desktop, even something as simple as putting a new icon on it, we tell all three of these groups a good month in advance. And then remind them in an e-mail just before it happens.

McCrory:

The head of Information Technology has to be someone who can communicate effectively and understands the need for it. I see a lot of my peers missing that point totally—that without communications, technology will encounter a lot of barriers.

(To put the following comment in context, the conversation was held a week before the launch of the Windows 2000 operating system.)

Cavallo:

I'll give you an example. I want to put Windows 2000 in our enterprise as fast as possible. But right now, we need to go through a process of building our business case and sharing with our key businesses why we think they should go through another upgrade, even though we just upgraded everybody over the last fourteen months.

A lot of technology managers would just say, Okay, we're going to roll out Windows 2000 starting February 15 with Finance first and then this group and then that group. Dictating to people instead of listening to them and working with them. I believe dictating technology can be disastrous, so we spend time talking to our customers, looking at their business plans, matching technology needs to business objectives, and helping executives see how technology can help them realize their goals more quickly and more cost-effectively.

McCrory:

What we've done has been a rousing success for Charlotte that goes way beyond just improving the technology. And that's what we were aiming for— not technology for the sake of technology, but technology with a bottom-line goal.

Mayor McCrory and his team started with a sense of the benefits that might be reaped by making Charlotte a technology showcase. The effort has added powerfully to the economic success of the city. IBM now has a major operation there. So does Sun Microsystems. In part because of the technology climate the city had created, Microsoft selected Charlotte for our major technical support center serving the whole East Coast, and we now have fifteen hundred people based there—up from zero only five years before. And the number is growing.

Downtown Charlotte is home to a heavy concentration of high-tech companies. The city is growing, it's pumped, and it's prospering.

Technology leadership starts at the top.

CHAPTER 3

*Every chief executive should look for a chief
information officer under the age of fifteen.*

—TOM PETERS
(who hopes you will not take him literally)

The More Heterogeneous the Technology Environment, the More Inefficient the Organization

When it comes to choosing hardware and software, too often the view is that everyone needs to roll their own, that every manager in the organization needs the freedom to select the items most suitable for the particular challenges of his or her operations.

It's a widespread view, containing a certain amount of logic and a certain amount of simple wrongheadedness.

And it can be a very political issue.

One of the great cries of many is for a completely heterogeneous technology environment: Every manager gets to pick what he thinks does the job best. So one unit has an IBM mainframe and an Oracle database, the next one has a Compaq mainframe and Microsoft applications, and some other part of the company has all Lotus software. Each one has chosen what appeared to be the best of breed for their precise jobs.

It's obvious that the more technologically heterogeneous the organization, the more complex it is to manage, the more difficult to move data around, and the more expensive. Complexity is the enemy of good management, effective control—and, in these highly competitive times, the enemy of the company's future prospects.

But if that's so obvious, how is it that so many organizations—very likely including yours—are still mired in the swamp of incompatible systems?

Any company that sets a course for working its way out of the swamp of complexity faces one compelling challenge: Is it possible to move to the high ground of homogeneity ... without turning every business-unit manager into an enemy of the Information Technology group?

The answer: It can be done.

One company that has succeeded in this effort is Scottish Power. Based in Glasgow, Scotland, and with twenty-four thousand employees, the Scottish Power group supplies energy to more than 7 million business and domestic customers across the United Kingdom and the western United States. Their annual sales totaling nearly £6.5 billion (U.S. $11 billion) rank the company as one of the top ten utilities in the world. And they are—surprise, surprise—considered to be a leading example of a company finding innovative e-business solutions.

David Jones, the company's group chief information officer, described the day of this conversation as "a good day in Glasgow because it hasn't rained." (Of course, based in the Seattle area, I understand a good deal about rainy climates.)

To set the stage for the conversation, I posed a question: Strategy is a necessary underpinning for technology solutions, but doesn't necessarily lead you to the concept of a homogeneous environment. What does it take to get a company to shift gears, wipe away the past, and begin the move toward a consistent technology?

David Jones found two powerful motivators. The company had different technology in each different division, and a variety of e-mail systems. Says Jones, "People were sick and tired of conversions.

Somebody would send out an Excel spreadsheet and get messages back saying, 'I haven't got Excel, send it to me in 1, 2, 3.' So they would end up making three or four different versions of the same bloody spreadsheet."

But what brought the issue to a head was deregulation of the British utility industry, leading to Scottish Power acquiring other companies. Top management began to recognize the need for some common technology standards. "We got lucky, thanks to deregulation." That gave IT the leverage it needed: "We had that problem, but we don't have it anymore."

Yet how do you convince business-unit managers to support a change like this?

David Jones:

> We began by looking at the IT infrastructure that new systems would operate under, and saw we were talking about an investment of something like £46 million [about U.S. $74 million]. I basically said to each of the individual business unit managers, "You don't need the hassle of worrying about these decisions and on top of that, if you act on your own, you're not going to have uniformity of e-mail and information flow. I can deliver this for you and guarantee the overall synergy, and I can do it for a total cost to the business of £20 million [U.S. $32 million] rather than 46 million."

What David heard back was the almost universal response:

> The business unit managers said, "But will you limit the choices of the applications I can use?" I was able to tell them, "No, we will absolutely guarantee you can choose any application you like and they will run on the infrastructure."
>
> The analogy I used was, "You can choose a 16-wheeler truck, a four-wheel drive, a normal motor car, a motorcycle, but you're all going to ride on one motorway. So let's make the motorway consistent and subcontract the building and the management of it to the people that really understand how."
>
> And that meant us—the in-house IT people.

It was an easy sell, we delivered, and there is now no question from any of the businesses that they would want to do it in any different way.

When all the organizations within a company can exchange information seamlessly, barriers come tumbling down.

Out of this experience, David Jones formulated his own notion of what it takes to be successful in this situation:

The key to success of business using IT doesn't come down to technology. It comes down to the major applications that underwrite the business processes.

I've found in my career that the only pushback you get is when you try to interfere with the businesses' choice of applications software, because that's the lifeblood of their organizations.

You simply say to the businesses, "I'm not going to tell you what to choose, and I won't even put any technical restraints on your choice." Once you've said that, then they relax. They're quite happy to let you adopt a common standard across the businesses.

If someone chooses an application that happens to run on a different operating system than you're managing in your infrastructure, if somebody chooses a major application that doesn't run on your IT infrastructure, you've got a simple call to make. You either introduce that as part of your underlying IT infrastructure component, or you port the application [i.e., taking a software application designed to run under one operating system, and "translating" it to run under another, so it becomes usable in the company's technology environment].

The only requirements we have for the application vendors is that we have a common form of information exchange, because we want consistency of data right across all the different systems even when they flow from one operating division to another.

The bottom line was that the business units said, It sounds like a very sensible thing to do, you're not restricting our applications, go ahead and do it. And we did.

. . .

In this era of outsourcing, a lot of companies have opted out of the David Jones solution, preferring to turn the challenge of fixing a homogeneity problem over to a contractor.

As you've no doubt heard and read, a new approach has been gaining popularity in dealing with suppliers, especially in the area of technology. And it's this: Whittle down your suppliers to a much more limited number. Select the best of breed in each of your four or five or so technology categories, and choose companies that have demonstrated they can work well with each other. Then hold each of these few vendors accountable to a new level of responsibility— not just selling you product, but adding value.

Why go outside for this? One answer is suggested by Archie Kane, the group executive director of Lloyds TSB plc, that venerable U.K. financial institution familiarly known as Lloyds Bank; (the "TSB" was added as the result of a merger with Trustee Savings Bank). His reasoning for going outside—

Archie Kane:
> We didn't think we had the resource or the skill and competence to do it. And if we had to do it, we were going to have to invest so much time, effort, and resource that it would become a life-form of its own. Why do that when you can call on a strategic supplier who has done it in a number of cases with a number of other firms?

Resisting this idea, some IT executives still feel, If I don't keep multiple vendors working against each other, the ones I've kept will soon take advantage of me because they'll know I have no choice. It follows the old adage of "Don't put all your eggs in one basket" that early generations learned at their mothers' knees, and it was a not uncommon argument back in the seventies and eighties that still hangs on in too many quarters.

In his years at Texaco, Ed McDonald ultimately became their most senior information technology leader, earning the eminent title of chief architect. A long-time friend as well as business colleague, Ed sadly died just prior to the scheduled publishing of this book. His views support this position about limiting the number of suppliers.

Ed McDonald:

> *History has suggested if there isn't constant competition, you become lethargic and forget that you have to earn the privilege of being a supplier every day. Now I would argue that today, because technology is so important, it becomes visible to the customer when a supplier takes it for granted.*
>
> *And as for vendors taking advantage of the position of an exclusive relationship with you, there is so much skin in the game that it mitigates some of the risk that may have been there in the past.*

Information Technology departments have purposely set up their purchasing so one supplier would compete with another for every application. Well, let's face it, they have a strong argument on their side: Look what happened to IBM loyalists in the 1980s, when the company forgot the customer and took us all for granted.

(To be honest, more than one customer would say today that they believe Microsoft is in the same position, and believe we're going to become another IBM-of-the-eighties, that we will take our customers for granted. I understand the fear; everything I know about the company after ten years of working with Gates, Ballmer, Herbold, and Raikes tells me that Microsoft is so intently focused on customer needs that we'd be one of the last companies to make that mistake. Sure—a clearly biased opinion; take it for what it's worth.)

Reducing the number of technology vendors to a very few who you work very closely with—when possible, a single one in each technology category—makes a great deal of sense.

. . .

When it comes to e-mail, the reason most companies have a multiplicity of incompatible systems isn't hard to fathom. The experience at Texaco was typical. "We were early adopters of electronic mail," says Ed McDonald. "People recognized the value of being able to interact with colleagues. We have a great deal of skill within the company, but we don't have a lot of depth—we would tend to have one or two people who were experts in any particular area, so those folks have to be available to the whole company."

The telephone wasn't particularly effective: "Somebody is on assignment in London and wants to talk to somebody who's on assignment in Indonesia, and it's hard to find a time when it's convenient to talk."

The motivation for using e-mail was there, but that need led to what Ed McDonald calls "a classic example." He explains—

> One group was running a mainframe-based mail system, some were using an old mail system from Digital, some were using PC systems, some were using Lotus. The Data General people had brought in their own mail software for the refineries. We had ccMail installed in Europe.
>
> Then Amoco and IBM developed a mainframe-based e-mail system on this virtual machine platform called PROFS, and the corporation decided after seeing everybody else using it that we needed to be a PROFS user as well, so we put the PROFS system up.

In all, Texaco had thirteen different e-mail systems running simultaneously. Many combinations couldn't communicate with each other, couldn't transfer documents. "And if they could, it was complicated, and documents were lost. People just gave up."

Texaco was spending a significant amount of money annually for products that attempted to interconnect the disparate systems, yet the communications headaches continued.

But the biggest motivator, Ed says, was "our belief that it's very important for every employee in Texaco to have access to every other employee so that the informal networks can grow and flourish and help us to be a differentiated company."

Still, solving the problem was no picnic.

> We evaluated the situation to decide what characteristics we needed in a company-wide mail system, and we found that none of the systems we were using met the need. We talked to Oracle about the system they were thinking of doing. We talked to Lotus about what their plans were for ccMail and Lotus Notes. We talked to Novell because we had Novell networks in at the time as well. And we talked to Microsoft.
>
> Microsoft seemed to be the only ones that were interested in hearing what we thought was a set of requirements for this environment. As a result, we got more involved and ended up working with them as one of the companies they looked to for guidance on designing the program that became the Microsoft Exchange e-mail product. There were six or eight of us around the table at the very beginning, working with the executive in charge of the product, Brian Valentine, Senior Manager Elaine Sharp, and their team.
>
> The systems that were currently installed at Texaco were not scalable, they couldn't be audited, they couldn't be used to transact business on a basis that we were comfortable with. In particular, we needed a system that could guarantee delivery, provide a report that a message was received, and handle mail marked to be privately delivered so we could be certain it would be delivered only to the person to whom it was addressed.
>
> We also needed an archiving mechanism so that the mail system was not just to transport but also a repository for knowledge and information.
>
> Brian and his team seemed to understand all of those issues, even when they were doubtful they could deliver 100 percent of everything we talked about.
>
> One of the reasons the program came out late was because we actually ended up discovering some rather significant shortfalls. Brian said, "It's better to put it out right than it is to put it out on time. If we have to rewrite this, we're going to do it." He took a lot of heat internally for that.

Okay, I think a disclaimer is necessary here. Though Ed McDonald has become a friend over the years, it would have been stupid to ask him for a testimonial. He offered the following entirely on his own, unprompted.

> *In the end Microsoft certainly delivered a scalable, well-architected messaging environment that meets the marketplace needs. We're basically 100 percent an Exchange shop now. The only other systems we have left at this point are a couple of other mail installations in some of our very small Latin American locations where the connectivity is not so good.*
>
> *We paid for the changeover and the new system within six months. It was more than a million dollars a year in savings, plus a multimillion-dollar physical saving—and that's just the cost saving. The real value is the fact that we have enhanced our ability for the company to have a free flow and exchange of ideas, concepts, and knowledge across boundaries, independent of time and space.*

Archie Kane of Lloyds TSB recognized the same problem about the multitude of e-mail systems. He calls this "an absolutely classic problem which virtually every company I've dealt with or talked to has had," which comes about when "each department, each business-unit manager, has described the technology that he wants for his own unit."

His prescription: Tackle the problem by establishing a working team made up of all the IT directors of the key business units or areas. Then keep driving them until "they agree on standards in those areas where it is simply just not sensible to go your own way. And that's on things like e-mail, telecommunications, networks, and desktop."

At Lloyds TSB, the team is called the Group IT Committee, and, as with the chief information officer of Charlotte, Kane has made a point of *not* serving as the chairman, so it won't appear that management is dictating to the group; instead, the members select a chairman themselves. Important work, Kane believes: "It is absolutely imperative that the different parts of the company agree on standards."

.   .   .

The problem of a too complex computing environment certainly isn't limited just to e-mail. Texaco had the same kind of headaches with desktop machines, and with networking.

Ed McDonald:

> I think just in our Information Technology Department, it turned out we had something like seventeen different manufacturers of PCs in a single eight-story building alone. That was carrying individual personal computing a little too personal. It was a group decision that maybe we needed a little more consistency.
>
> We also had four or five competing local area network technologies—the complexity that develops naturally within a complex business. A thousand points of light weren't all pointing in the same direction and we weren't getting enough light to illuminate anything.
>
> So we needed to put some architectural organization around what we were doing. But that brings a potential for there to be winners and losers among the business units—everybody wants their own architecture to be the one that becomes the standard. In this situation it's extremely important that you approach the problem in a collaborative fashion rather than a cooptive or preemptive fashion.

This time Texaco organized a different kind of group.

> We pulled together a council made up of the information officers in each of the business units to talk about what this diversity was costing us. Those discussions began with, Where is our pain, where are we spending the most money and getting the least results?

The answers provided a road map for launching the effort to create a homogeneous computing environment throughout the global corporation.

.   .   .

The difficulties when one organization finds itself using a great variety of desktop machines and a multitude of networking standards—what was true at Texaco was also true at Lloyds TSB.

Archie Kane:

> We realized we had the burgeoning problem that many, many large companies have: a proliferation of the desktop. We had every shape and size of desktop device you could possibly imagine. A large number of them networked, using different network standards and all sorts of different application suites, which couldn't communicate with one another in any meaningful form.
>
> But in addition to that, we realized the total cost of ownership of this particular environment was just getting out of control.

What did they do? Taking a different path than Scottish Power and their in-house solution, Archie Kane picked an outside supplier. The company had already drastically reduced the number of technology suppliers on their list, for reasons described above. They chose a contractor from the newly limited group of suppliers, and handed them the task of taking over and managing the Lloyds TSB desktop environment.

"We redid initially about fifteen thousand desktops and then we increased it to twenty thousand, then twenty-five thousand, and now we have a rolling program." Each department or employee has a limited choice: "They can have the desktop or the laptop, and the machines come with a standard application suite," in addition to other application suites approved by the line management and by a senior manager in IT to serve special requirements.

Incidentally, unlike many U.S. firms, Lloyds TSB is "quite strict" about employees using the computers for personal matters; it's considered a disciplinary offense. E-mailing jokes or material "of a salacious nature" is a major offense.

With standardization, Lloyds TSB now has people "communicating right across the organization." The only way that happens, Archie Kane maintains, is to "pull the key players into the center and keep after them until they agree on standards."

Texaco's technology leader offers a rule of thumb for this—

Ed McDonald:

> *The underlying lesson is that when managers are left to their own devices, any effective technology will tend to diversify, and that will result in a highly complex structure that will be difficult to scale and to maintain so it's always reliable.*
>
> *Instead, we need to follow the familiar principle of management called KISS—keep it simple, stupid. It applies here as it does in other things that undue complexity results in undue cost. The world is complex enough on its own, we don't need to introduce any additional levels of complexity into it.*

Even before you can begin contemplating drastic changes in your organization's technology scheme, there needs to be—as I point out repeatedly in these pages—an underlying, comprehensive technology strategy. The best of companies figure this out for themselves.

Some years ago Texaco formed a council specifically for looking at technology strategy. Called the Information Strategy Group, it was made up not of technologists but people from the business side—in this case, the business unit heads.

Ed McDonald:

> *The Strategy Group was charged with the responsibility of making sure that the solutions and technologies we were bringing into play were indeed those that would make sense for the business and not just for the technologists. We wanted people to say, "Here are our drivers from a business strategy standpoint."*

Referring to me, Ed recalled the time that I came to one of the first meetings of the group and talked about . . .

> **Technology as a business driver rather than as technology for technology's sake.**
>
> That was a key item for us because it helped us make sure that we kept the emphasis on the right side of the equation.
>
> The rationale for forming the Information Strategy Group was really something that would seem so logical that you would on the one hand wonder how come every company hasn' t figured it out, but on the other hand would realize it is something people really are missing. It appears to be one of those things that everybody says, "Oh yes, of course," when they hear it, but that most companies haven' t figured out to do yet.
>
> If you' re in a business where you' re the dominant player and the margins are adequate, and you' re able to get by without being really efficient, you can just do business as usual, and you may not be forced into recognizing this requirement. In our case, we were forced into it by the competitive pressure of being in a low-margin business.

The bottom line message is simple: Homogeneity is too important to ignore.

In the end, I do care which messaging system or networking system you choose, but I care even more that you choose only *one* of each for your entire organization. One system is better than two or several, even if it's not Microsoft's. The added complexity of doing things the traditional way, and the added costs, are so obvious as arguments against multiple systems that the conclusion is inescapable: the more homogeneous the technology environment, the better, in myriad ways.

The more you limit that number of systems, the better you will answer your organization's technology needs.

CHAPTER 4

We live in a world that doesn't have many noes.
If you can dream it, you can do it.

—DENNIS ECK

Making Information Technology
the Business of Management

Earlier I argued that this new era of computing, this e-business/Digital Revolution era, is fundamentally different in the relationship of technology to the organization from any previous era of computing. The earlier technologies were like equipping a home with indoor plumbing: It saved time and made the experience more pleasant—you could take a bath in a warm room, with all the hot water you wanted, and so on.

But in this new era, technology becomes a catalyst for changing the business itself.

It follows that the people who are responsible for managing something that changes the very business you are in clearly have a strategic role to play. Question: Should these people be from the technology side of the organization, or from the business side? And a related question: If from the business side, how can they adapt to the needs of running a technology operation?

Thorny questions . . . and ones that not very many companies have successfully answered. The experience of two quite different companies—Marriott Hotels and Lloyds TSB Bank—illustrate two quite different yet successful approaches.

At Lloyds TSB Bank, Archie Kane is a too rare example of a person with one foot in each camp—a business person who is also knowledgeable about technology. He holds graduate degrees in accountancy and business, yet came to be a groundbreaker in reshaping attitudes toward technology at the very conservative, very traditional Lloyds TSB. How does that happen?

Archie Kane:

I was not a technology professional: I was more of a general business guy. In my early years at the bank, I moved out of finance and ran business operations, things like a credit card business, a mortgage business, a money transmission business, the life insurance business, a savings business—running each as a business operations manager.

All of those operations to a degree are IT dependent. A credit card business is very dependent on computer and communications technologies; money transmission is hugely dependent, on a systemic level. So I was constantly engaged with the central IT functions—sometimes positively, sometimes in an arm wrestle. I was constantly talking to the IT people and often getting a bit frustrated because I never felt they were coming to me with the sorts of creative solutions that would solve the business problems I had presented them. I was constantly looking at IT and thinking, If I could have a solution in this area or that area, it would help me. Where are the clever ideas? What would it take for them to come up with more creative solutions?

I have always been inquisitive in terms of trying to pick up what IT was doing. So I gained quite a bit of experience and knowledge from the business-user point of view.

How deep a technical level did that involve? For Archie, it was at the level of keeping the bank's operations current with the latest technological innovations.

As an example, I can remember back in the early nineties being engaged in all sorts of debates with the IT function over why they weren't providing us solutions based on object-oriented programming, because I could see a business value. What they were grappling with was that it was really in its infancy and it was very difficult to apply. But it was typical of the kind of debates with IT that you need to stay involved in.

The real awakening came when Kane was asked to take over the Lloyds TSB division called IT and Operations, which includes the whole information technology function.

Because I had already been through this period of dealing with IT from the outside, I understood what a business manager wanted from IT, and what IT was actually providing, and they were two different things.

I was also fortunate in having to wrestle with the IT integration problems in some mergers the bank did, and from that it became even more apparent to me that there are some kinds of problems you can't let the IT guys wrestle with on their own. When it's a business problem, you can't have the IT guys going to a smoke-filled room and coming out with an IT solution.

What's the road a company needs to take to align IT more closely with the needs of the business?

I defy any major company nowadays not to have technology-based competencies such as the quality of your data, how you use that data, how you analyze it, and how you deploy it as a strategic competence. And if you try and identify those other things in which you must develop a core competence, and you're rigorous about it, you'll list such things as getting close to the customer and managing your employees well. And as soon as you acknowledge these things as essential core competencies, you begin to see that technology is the fundamental blood that runs in the veins of all these elements.

I've found that people who've spent all their life in technology come to have quite a narrow career path and therefore struggle when they come out of the technology arena into top management. Top management is all about managing the world of ambiguity. It's not binary, it's not yes or no, it's all about how many uncertainties can I identify.

In my experience a lot of technology people don't accumulate much experience in dealing with life that way. This puts a lot of the burden on the businesspeople, to develop enough understanding of technology. That's the only way they can make sure IT will present them with solutions that answer the business problems. Technology has to be seen as a management issue.

One of the world's premier motel/hotel chains, now called Marriott International, got its start in the 1930s when the founder, J. Willard Marriott, who had begun in business with a roadside root beer stand, noticed a lot of people setting out on a trip were coming by his food place to pick up something to eat on the airplane. He saw an opportunity for the airlines to provide a great service to their passengers by offering food in flight. The airlines quickly agreed, and the business, you might say, quickly took off.

The "motor hotels," as they were first called, came later.

Maybe it has something to do with this visionary streak of its founder that Marriott was among the first hotel companies to recognize the business opportunity offered by the Internet. This was in 1996, practically the pioneer days of business on the Web.

The company's approach, though, hardly fit what would become the usual pattern. Instead of telling the CIO, "Get us a Web site," management pulled a youngster out of the business side, a marketing guy named Mike Pusateri, who had no technical background and would have to learn everything he needed on the fly.

Then they created a separate unit for him because they were afraid the traditional businesses wouldn't be as motivated to deal with what promised to be something of a gut-wrenching change. And it was.

Mike didn't see the Internet as some kind of technical magic act that you turned over to a bunch of HTML programmers. He saw it as a great new marketing tool, and he figured if Marriott got in early, the company could leverage it to their competitive advantage.

A hotel room is like an airplane seat: it's perishable. The closer you get to a day that a given room is unbooked, the more motivated you are to book it. Yesterday's leftover newspapers can be recycled, but yesterday's empty hotel room is an opportunity lost forever. If you can sell that otherwise empty room, most of the money you collect goes right to the bottom line. Pusateri built a system to sell the rooms online, offering special deals that got better as you got closer to the date. Want a room tomorrow night? How does $85 sound?

On average, Marriott was able to increase its revenues by several dollars per room, per night. Across the entire chain worldwide, that came to a very significant hunk of change.

Too many companies turn over the creation of their Internet sites to Web design experts who have mastered the technology but don't understand the company's business equation. And when the site doesn't measure up to expectations, the designers may get the blame, even though it isn't their fault.

I've always believed that if you told a joke to George and George didn't get it, there was no point explaining. If you have to explain, George will never find it funny.

I insist that same reasoning does not apply here, so I'm going to expound the underlying message, even if you've already grasped it:

> **Today, information technology can't be left to the specialists. It's too bloody important; the future of your organization very probably depends on the technology choices made today.**

Traditionally the thinking has been that the IT Department had its own IT budget and it had to make the business case for large IT purchases through Finance and on to senior management. Sometimes that took the form of, "We've got this much computer capacity, the business will grow X percent next year, we'll need more computer capacity, it will cost X dollars, please approve." And sometimes it took the form of, "Here's this new technology, and here's why if we install it, you'll get X payback." In both the cases you had IT organizations making the business case and justifying it in their budget.

And in many organizations still today, the IT spend is looked on as a target you set as a percentage of something—"IT shouldn't be more than 3 percent of the operating budget," or some percent of net revenues, or whatever—some arbitrary percentage that let the managers feel they weren't overspending or underspending on IT.

And of course there are consulting organizations that will come in, look at your IT spend, compare it to others in your industry, and report to you on whether you're doing well, poorly, or in between.

The general theme has been that this is all the responsibility of the IT group. I argue quite the opposite point of view. Giving IT the responsibility for the business case makes the assumption that they can somehow be held accountable to it—why would you give someone responsibility for some business matter if you're not going to hold them accountable?

Yet IT can't be held accountable for the business case because the bulk of the benefit from technology comes as a result of some business manager's decision. Business managers should have the responsibility because they ultimately should be held accountable for making the changes that technology allows them to make.

Furthermore, if you look at most cost studies for IT spend, there's very little after-the-fact audit. You have this big effort, it's supposed to reap a very attractive payoff. And three years out no one's even looked back at whether there was any payoff at all. Or else—"My procedure says I need a cost-benefit study to make the case so I have to attach one." But no one is held accountable. Most of these methodologies are just a waste, just a way to fill a CFO's accounting square. All this just adds to the silliness.

We have to change our thinking, stop the nonsensical approach to cost justification, and simply hold business managers accountable for making the changes needed to result in the payoff of the IT investment. And hold IT accountable for managing IT costs as efficiently as possible. And most of all, make technology expenses a business decision.

The way technology decisions are made at Microsoft is, admittedly, a very special case: We're a technology company with a distinctive appreciation for the issues at stake, and with particular knowledge of the underlying principles.

Even so, we sometimes don't get it right even within our own company. A few years ago, Bill Gates remarked to a group of Microsoft executives that as leading users of technology, our company probably ran on significantly less paperwork than other companies our size. And he asked the question, "How many different forms does it take to run Microsoft?"

He heard the number and went ballistic. When he climbed down from the ceiling, he said something like, "I want us to look hard core at all our internal processes, and dramatically reduce that number."

This wasn't just a paperwork measure. To some degree a form is a representation of a process; the form exists because some process requires it. Or *appears* to require it.

Today the number of forms at Microsoft has been reduced to some fraction of the former amount.

But Bill didn't let the story end there; he pushed the idea one huge step further. Today the forms we still use are *online*. And that didn't happen by taking the paper forms and translating them into identical electronic versions; each was redesigned in a user-friendly way, taking maximum advantage of the conveniences offered by an Intranet. In many cases I don't have to fill in items like my employee number, my department, and my boss's name; items already available in a corporate database are usually filled in automatically. And when I click Okay or Send, the form goes directly to the appropriate department.

"But hold on," you say. "How about all those legal forms that require a physical signature? Surely you still have to do those in hard copy, right?"

Some, yes. But not as many as you might expect.

Example: The Securities and Exchange Commission requires that every director, officer, and senior manager of every publicly held company must once a year sign a form in which they in effect certify that they are honest and true and worthy of trust—I have paid my taxes and will pay them this year, I have not declared bankruptcy and have no plans to do so, et cetera. It's mandated by the government that these forms must be signed and filed by our Legal Department.

But when Microsoft checked with the SEC, the answer came back, Yes, you may use an electronic version of this form.

So once a year now, I receive an e-mail that contains the entire form. The instructions say something like, If you agree with the statements contained herein, click here to send an e-mail acknowledgment.

I read the form, point and click . . . and it's done.

Many of the forms that logic and experience said would have to stay in hard copy, didn't. And all because our CEO pushed people to use technology in a more effective way.

Here was a case of a CEO involving himself in a level of his company that CEOs don't ordinarily dirty their hands with.

Travel expense reporting. Every businessperson who travels would love to know who started the present system so they could throttle the guy, or at least demand to know what on earth he could have been thinking.

Almost every U.S. company has the same rule, and many overseas have a comparable one: any expense over $25 needs a receipt. Sound familiar? You collect all these scraps of paper everywhere you go. Most of them from a typical trip are taxicab receipts. When was the last time you didn't get a blank receipt from the taxi driver? He never fills it out but gives you a blank to do it yourself, and will even give you extra ones if you ask. And you *must* submit those receipts, even if they're in your own handwriting.

It's so bizarre. I'm visiting some corporation and I say, I bet your rule is that you need receipts for every expense of $25 or more, right? The answer is yes 99.9 percent of the time. (The few exceptions include some government operations; one state in the Northeast—I had to promise I would not say which one—requires receipts for any expense over *$6*.)

When you get back from the trip, you fill out the form, sign it, and attach the receipts—which, of course, have to be in the same order as the items on the form, to make it easier for the accountant who has to check the whole thing. But first it has to go to your boss; you know what a pain this is because you probably get a stack from your own workers. Every Thursday at 4:00, or every time you need to take a break and do something mindless, you pick up the stack and zip through them, glancing at the bottom line to make sure somebody didn't spend one night in Pittsburgh and submit an expense sheet for $10,000, and then you sign them without further ado.

Of course, from time to time, there will be that dreaded call from Accounting—you've been on the road in Europe for two weeks, you've spent $8,000 out of your own pocket, but you're missing a receipt for $27.50 and they won't pay anything until you find it.

Why should those receipts be necessary? Because Accounting needs them. Why? Because it's an IRS requirement.

We checked with the IRS. The requirement is that you have receipts for expenses of $75 or more. Virtually the whole of corporate America is bogged down in paperwork that nobody really needs.

At Microsoft, we changed the rule—submit receipts only for expenses of $75 or more. The IRS also said employees did not have to physically sign their expense reports.

Wonderful. We now do 95 percent of the process online. Yes, hotel and airline receipts and the like still have to go to Accounting, but the rest of it is done with an online form. When you've finished filling it out, one click and it goes to your boss.

What the boss sees is a summary with only four data elements—where you went, the dates, the purpose (I always put "business"; nobody complains), and the total. If he wants more information, he can click Reply to send an e-mail back and ask for it. If he's satisfied, he simply clicks his acknowledgment and, presto, Accounting gets his or her approval to pay.

Guess what. My boss, Jeff Raikes, has better things to do. (I describe Jeff as the man responsible for everything in Microsoft that goes on outside of Redmond; his official title is group vice president for worldwide sales, marketing and services.) He has always sent the expense reports forward with a scan and a click. That part isn't new; I've surveyed managers around the world and know that approvals are mostly done at a glance.

So here's Microsoft, probably the most audited company on the face of the earth, with IRS people living here full-time, and we're no longer hung up on that cumbersome processing of paper that everybody else has been deluded into thinking is an IRS requirement.

I spoke about this silly travel receipts business in a talk I gave to the government managers and executives of one midwestern state. Afterward one lady came up and said, "You know, my full-time job is checking these damn pages with all these receipts, and you are absolutely right." She was fired up about the subject. "The only reason this isn't changing is the people in charge. The working-level people, they know it's stupid, they do it every day. But the manager of receipts and travel expenses sees his or her career being threatened. They're the ones holding back, not the working level."

On the nose.

But old habits die hard. In previous eras of computing, technology decisions were based on traditional cost-benefit studies—which most of the time resulted in attempts to quantify the unquantifiable. Time-consuming efforts to make Finance happy with these silly reports.

The old approaches said, You do some kind of productivity analysis or whatever, and show that the technology purchase you're proposing will save time, save labor, save cost. The studies were focused on tactical stuff like increasing typing speed or saving paper clips.

Some of the statistical approaches that were and still are put forward should be taken with a grain of salt. You might find in one book a claim that 80 percent of some company's growth was due to office automation. Or, in another, that a company benefited to the tune of $60-plus million in one year due to technology improvements. Or a calculation showing how automation can produce a return of 800,000 percent over a single 12-month period!

With authoritative claims like this being made in prominent places, is it any wonder so many of us were misguided for so long, and happily subscribed to this kind of nonsense as a way of gaining buy-in for technology purchases? (My use of the word "us" here is highly appropriate: Before joining Microsoft, I spent seven-plus years advising companies about such matters, on the staff of consulting firm Ernst & Young.)

Simply stated, we were putting the responsibility on the wrong people to make the case for the expenditure. The studies were valid enough in their own way. But in today's climate, that kind of self-justification from the company's technology group continues putting the focus on the wrong issues.

It's the CEO or business-unit leader who must not only take responsibility, but also assume the responsibility for demonstrating that the investment will pay off.

Ankara, Turkey—1997.

This principle of management appropriating the authority to make decisions about technology applies as well in the public domain, and that fact once struck me pointedly in a most unexpected locale.

I was sitting in a meeting with the education minister of Turkey. He and his top staff were sharing with me the initiatives they were hoping to pursue for taking advantage of the Digital Revolution to position their country economically at a different level.

They spoke about Turkey's 65 million people, over half of whom are less than twenty years old. And they had looked at what had happened with India's investments in certain fields, how that country had become an intellectual supplier for Europe and the United States in areas like software.

The minister hoped that Turkey would be able to invest heavily—"over-invest," to use his term—in building a technical infrastructure, networking the schools of the entire nation, training the teachers . . . He had a dream of catching the kids while they still had enough years to go in the classroom, and building over a few years a technology base for the country. He had a dream of one day being able to say, We're super–well networked and we offer an intellectual talent pool that's on a par with any.

The minister and his staff hoped that if they could do it right, the country's graduates could land great high-tech jobs without the problem India is having, where so many of the young people are leaving the country. And they could see the possibility of outdoing other countries that are trying to ratchet up the technology level of their workforce by making a big point of their proximity to Europe.

I listened, awed by the enthusiasm and vision of these people and realizing that unlike the U.S., where education decisions are made state by state, county by county, city by city, Turkey and its education leaders truly could frame a national commitment.

Whether they will actually achieve this remains to be seen. But the fact that high government officials were thinking in that strategic way impressed me.

These days when I encounter corporate managers who haven't yet grasped that information technology is the business of management, I always remember those educators in Turkey. A powerful lesson.

These examples serve to illustrate one simple but powerful principle. A company's Information Technology or Management Information Systems group manages costs, not benefits. So—

Managers need to take the reins of technology, driving technology decisions that are based on solid business needs.

IT investments prove most valuable only when the decisions are made by business management, to serve the needs of the business.

We've got a six- to eight-person team
working on Internet progress in each
of GE's businesses. Every business
is coming in May with their new game plan
[based around the Internet].

—JACK WELCH, in March 1999

A Business Plan Not Based on Technology Isn't a Plan, It's an Illusion

The idea that you should integrate systems planning with business planning is something consultants have been espousing for years. But the reality in most companies is that these are still very distinct processes, done by separate groups. Okay, the planning may happen in parallel, at the same time of the year, but the only real link comes when everybody finishes their plans and all the budgets are rolled up together, including the technology budget. Then every manager and executive argues about what percentage of the technology dollars they can get for their own business unit.

That's not what integration means. It means simultaneously developing the two plans as an integrated process—the technology plan based on the goals expressed in the business plan, the business plan tailored to take maximum advantage of what technology can make possible.

A business planning process that's integrated to the extent I argue it should be means there will not be a plan from any business unit that doesn't integrate technology as a critical factor in delivering to goal.

But to develop a business plan integrated at this level and done in time, the business-unit managers must have a level of involvement with IT much greater than in the past.

That's a challenge, sure. And it means changing some familiar, comfortable ways of operating. A big payoff comes when your technology people spot some new trend like voice recognition and the company is able to jump on the bandwagon early, well ahead of competitors. Because powerful new technology tools will keep coming faster, and faster, and faster, every time you make one leap to keep up with technology, you're going to have to make another one shortly after just to stay competitively abreast. It no longer makes sense—if it ever really did—to sit back and wait for the others to try out the new stuff so you can see whether it's any good before you commit. Do that, and by the time you leap, all the other guys will already be on to the next step.

If this integration is at the level I suggest, the stand-alone technology plan all but disappears, and the technology budget becomes a piece of each business-unit budget. So the age-old debate about whether this year's technology budget should be 6 percent of the total budget, or whether it should be some other figure, disappears. In its place come more useful debates within each unit, at each P&L level, about the need for certain technologies. The discussions then turn on needs and benefits, not on the allocation of some arbitrary budget figure.

At Texaco, Ed McDonald saw a dramatic shift in how technology was viewed by the business side. What they called a "Governance Council," organized in 1993 and made up of business-unit managers, has provided a forum in which new technology ideas can be presented, and where technology needs can be aired.

It wasn't always like this. Much more than most companies, Texaco managers had a good reason for being reluctant to embrace new technology.

A short economics lesson about the oil and gas industry: We all complain now and then about the cost of filling the tank at the gas pump; the reality is that the retail gasoline business has the lowest margins of nearly any commodity. And because gasoline is such a huge volume product, variations in price can be devastating. As Ed McDonald describes it, "They don't worry about the size of the margin, they worry about the *sign* of the margin." Translation: A profit of half a cent per gallon can turn in a hurry to a loss of half a cent per gallon. And that negative number, multiplied by the vast number of gallons pumped at filling stations every single day, can hit hard on the company's bottom line. With those razor-thin margins, if something changes and the company doesn't react quickly enough, they can be giving away a significant number of dollars.

Because of that characteristic of the market, new, innovative approaches that would add any appreciable fixed cost to what was already a high fixed-cost business had long been a very hard sell. It makes sense to adopt change slowly when you have to be right every time, and managers were naturally hesitant to take a risk that could cut into the margin. So it had long been difficult for the Information Technology group even to put in demonstration programs that could provide validation for a new concept.

In the mid-eighties, for example, the Information Technology group assisted Retail Marketing in setting up a filling station for employees in the parking lot within their complex, and tested a concept they had been working on with some of the pump manufacturers: a card reader at the pump, so customers could get gas themselves without needing to walk inside to pay. The test was very successful, but the company made a business decision not to pursue the concept.

In the end, Texaco's competitors introduced pumps just like the ones that the Texaco IT people had been in the forefront of developing.

It took a new chairman to see a way around that dilemma. The world of businesspeople in one camp and IT in another effectively came to an end with the organization of the company's Governance Council.

Ed McDonald:

We develop our technology strategy now as part of developing our business strategy, and it is done by what amounts to a board of governors made up of the people who are running the businesses. IT is getting earlier buy-in now. That's showing in ways like the company being much more aggressive with our move into electronic business. And in our exploration and deepwater production areas, many of which are highly dependent on the information technology component, we're getting much better at anticipating the kinds of changes happening.

Through the forum of the Governance Council, the business leaders are actually presenting their basic strategies to the Information Technology groups and asking, "What are areas in this strategy where we could make significant inroads by using technology?"

In the reverse direction, the technology people are now able to say, "Here are interesting new technologies that seem to have applicability; how would they impact your strategy formulation?"

What does it take to get these kinds of changes started? It's different at each company, of course, but the Texaco experience offers some key lessons.

Texaco had a legacy to begin with because we had what we called the ICUT, the Improved Computer Utilization Team, that had been formed some twenty years ago. And by the by, the folks who put that together were all business-people, they weren't computer jocks. But brilliant—three of those who were on the committee at various points later in their careers became CEO of the company.

We were still working from the ICUT playbook. So it was almost a natural for us to say, "That's worked for us for a long time. Maybe we ought to make it a standing activity, building a strategy around our information technology to achieve a tighter coupling with our business strategy."

This isn' t just a budgeting exercise; we were actually looking for, How does the technology influence the business and how does the business influence the technology? A lot of these epiphanies occur as a result of "Necessity is the mother of invention."

We happened to have gone through a change in leadership. The fellow who is now the chief technology officer of the company and a vice president of our Strategic Planning Group had been based in Europe and also acting as the liaison to our Asian business. He came back as the general manager of information technology and from what he has seen out in the field, he said, "A lot of the problem we' re having is that we don' t have the ease of communication to the rest of the business that we need to have. I' d like to do something about it."

So it' s the right leadership at the right time, with the right environment. And a recognition of the need for having both effectiveness and efficiency in how you do business.

The CEO of a large insurance company made a comment to me about this modern approach to planning. He said, "We want the IT budget to reach a point where it's 100 percent of all operating expenses."

That was a way of expressing an attitude, of course—obviously not meant as a real-world goal. His point was that if you believe technology offers the most leverage of anything strategic you can do, the dream would be to spend all your money on it.

A business planning process that's fully integrated means that all business managers will today write their plans around how e-commerce and the Internet are integrated into the business. And that's what Jack Welch meant when he told every division head in General Electric to "bring me a business plan based around the Internet."

To get a business plan integrated with IT at this level, everybody from the midlevel managers up needs a degree of involvement with IT much greater than you've ever had in the past.

Here's another example of business planning, one on such a small scale that you may think I've gone a little weak-headed to include it. But this one delights me because, small as the operation is (and they don't get any smaller!), the story offers a prime example of using technology for a business solution.

Helen King, at age sixty-six, relaunched herself in the hotel industry. What happened was that she paid a visit to picturesque San Juan Island, in the Puget Sound, not far from Seattle and within sight of Victoria, on Vancouver Island, Canada. She fell in love with the place and decided she wanted to shift her business operations there.

"Business operations" overstates the case: Helen owned a twelve-room bed-and-breakfast on Monterey Bay, in Santa Cruz, California. After that visit to the Puget Sound, she dreamed of selling the Santa Cruz B&B and replacing it with one on the Island. But she could see big problems.

Helen King:
> *My primary goal was to build a place with two luxury suites and not have to have employees. Help is hard to get on the island and I really prefer doing it myself with just two guest suites in the house, two couples at a time as guests, and I live upstairs.*
>
> *I knew that no one would find me in this remote area with only two rooms, and I couldn't afford to advertise.*

A sensible business plan to meet Helen's goal would have been a challenge even for an expert. But in the end, her plan was straightforward.

> *A lot of guidebook authors won't even include you unless you've been in business for a year, and then you have to wait another year until the book*

*goes to publication. And when I say I couldn't afford to advertise, I couldn't
afford even advertising in Seattle, let alone nationally and globally.*

*So as far as getting the word out, I knew that I would have to use the
Internet. With it, I'd be able to cover the world. The thing about the Internet
is you get instant recognition.*

The problem faced by this retirement-age independent entrepre-
neur will have a familiar ring to many.

*I had a computer in Santa Cruz but it was mostly used by my front desk man-
ager for keeping track of reservations. I never had a chance to do anything
else with it and the whole idea was kind of scary for me. I went to the college up here when I moved to the island and took the beginners' computer
class. Twice.*

*At first I was intimidated by computers. Then I took some advanced
classes, and then finally I was ready to buy a computer and had a fellow on
the island install it.*

*I looked at some Web sites that I thought were attractive, and then picked
a graphic artist and we sat down together and worked out my site, and
revised it.*

The response was almost immediate. Helen opened "the Highland Inn of San Juan Island" in January 1998 with no rooms
reserved, and launched her new Web site at the same time. Within
a matter of weeks she was booked nearly full house for the entire
summer.

*Through the summer I had a booking rate in the high 80 percent range,
which is phenomenal for a first-year business.*

*By the time a customer calls, I don't spend extra time on the phone
because they know what rooms are available, they know the price and what
the inn has to offer, and I don't have to describe the rooms. So I really don't
spend any time selling anymore, all I do is take their name and address and
phone, the dates they want, and their credit card information.*

> *I discovered at the last big innkeepers' conference that most owners are not even bothering with brochures anymore.*
>
> *There's always more to learn, but I think I've gotten over the fear stage. I'm enjoying it now. In fact, I'd say I'm addicted. I can hardly wait to come down in the morning to see who sent me an e-mail, and it's the last thing I check at night.*

Helen King has guests coming not just from all over North America, but from Europe, Russia, Australia, even China—nearly every part of the world—to her little two-room inn on Puget Sound.

Ordinary planning challenges look minuscule beside the problems when the effort involves creating an e-commerce solution. Since shepherding Marriott International through that process in the early days of the Web, Mike Pusateri has moved on to become a senior VP of Proxicom, an Internet consulting business, which has given him the opportunity to draw broad conclusions about the challenges.

Mike Pusateri:

> *Companies have competencies in strategy, technology, and creative, but tend to keep these abilities in separate silos. Gradually they're learning how to get a technology person, a creative, and a business strategy person on the same team on a project.*
>
> *If you look at projects in a traditional firm, you've got IT on one side, and on the other side you've got the businessperson who is funding the project, setting strategy, looking at it in terms of earnings per share, ROI, and from the resource allocation standpoint—how are we going to fund this, and so on.*
>
> *Because they're operating in silos, it may not be till late in the project that they recognize, Hey, there's a big problem here. At Marriott, we had eleven brands, and the e-business project was the first time they all had to be on the same page. Suddenly Ritz Carlton is screaming, "We don't want to be anywhere near Marriott." So there was a whole logistics issue no one had ever dealt with before.*

> *Companies simply underestimate the planning process. Each effort requires a sponsor, some project management oversight, and some depth of knowledge of the particular function. Those are three distinctly different kinds of resources.*

A lot of people need to buy into an e-business effort before it can get off the ground.

> *You've got to get the CIO sponsorship, you've got to get the development VP to say he's willing to transfer funds and people from working on legacy systems to working on this.*
>
> *Then you go to Marketing, and it's the same thing. Are the resources going to come out of advertising? or where?*

Clearly Mike agrees on the troubles that arise when there is a lack of integrating technology and business planning. Another is finding the right people to man a project that has to be highly sensitive to both the business and the technological disciplines simultaneously.

> *Often the biggest mistake companies make is that they underestimate that whole process. They say, "Let's get started." But it's not that easy.*
>
> *Even once the executives have agreed to go ahead, that's still not the answer because who are they going to put on the project—are they people who know the first thing about the Web?*
>
> *There's a kind of musical chairs that goes on until the dust settles. The music starts playing, and everybody says, "I want to be part of this." A marketer comes in, full of enthusiasm, decides he doesn't belong there, he doesn't understand what it's all about. He figures, I'm not good at this, I could be a big failure here. Two weeks later he's gone back to his previous position.*
>
> *"Interactive marketing" used to mean direct mail, so naturally some of those people tend to jump in and want to be part of the Web operation, as well.*
>
> *Sometimes the company doesn't realize until two or three iterations later*

that the people they have on the Internet project are not qualified. So it
becomes a musical chairs syndrome.

You can't turn someone into a Web guru overnight.

Scottish Power's David Jones, in Research and Development for a
bank early in his career, witnessed that organization's very first computer being delivered.

David Jones:

> *It was called a mainframe even though it had a whole 2K of memory. It used*
> *magnetic tapes, paper tapes, card readers, and required a big staff of card-*
> *punch clerks to process the input data. There wasn't even an assembler in*
> *those days—we wrote in raw machine code.*

Starting as a software programmer, by the mid-1970s David was
managing the software support for Honeywell, which at the time
was something like number two after IBM. Since then he has
worked in Australia and in Los Angeles, has worked in the oil and
gas and constructions industries. In '95 he was hired to take over as
CIO at Scottish Power. His success there brought him the honor of
being named IT Director of the Year in Scotland for 1998.

One of the advantages he brought when he joined Scottish Power
was the vision to see how technology needed to enhance the business vision.

> *As we move more and more into the e-business revolution, it's not just a*
> *technology. One of my roles is to guide a way through for the business man-*
> *agers, especially saying to them, "Don't worry about the technology, let's*
> *worry about how we basically do things differently and better. We'll provide*
> *the technology to make it happen.'*

Fundamental to David's approach was this principle of making
technology a basic ingredient of business planning.

Part of that process involves taking a different attitude toward business planning in which technology isn't just a division that does a business plan like every other division, but technology being, if you will, a kind of under-structure for the entire business planning process—everybody taking technology into account.

In the end, technology is only there to deliver value as an enabling capability for the business. There is no point in spending money on technology if the business could then not take advantage of it to deliver business benefits far and above what's been spent on the technology.

IT is an investment like any other investment and you need to get a business benefit from it.

For IT to be an enabler, you need to understand what the business wants to do in the future, and therefore you need an IT strategic plan that becomes underpinning for the business strategic plan.

Even better: You go platinum if, as we've suggested, IT has a good relationship with the business and you do this together. Your IT enabling can actually enhance the business plan, the future business strategy.

It really becomes a tight fit between IT being an enabler to the business, and business delivering benefits from IT. And that really is the IT job, that's what their responsibility is. Delivering the technology is just routine, it's what IT people should do in their sleep, it's their day job.

The real IT role is using technology to add to the current and the future business strategy and business benefits.

And the way executives at Scottish Power see that now is different from the way it can be seen in a lot of other companies. It's certainly different than most utilities would see it and I think probably 75 percent of the U.K. companies don't see it that way, only 25 percent do. And we're one of those 25 percent.

Except for companies in some part of the high-tech world, technology in the past had always served a tactical function. David Jones agrees with me that e-commerce is unlikely to work unless it grows out of the *strategic* aspects of technology.

David Jones:

> I describe the new role of a technology leader as having a ponytail and san-
> dals on his feet, but dressed in a pinstriped suit. It's having your feet on the
> ground enough to say, "Okay, this is a great piece of technology, but how do
> I wrap it into a viable business plan that could have some probability of suc-
> ceeding and achieving some goal of the company?"
>
> IT is there as an enabler, it's there to effectively help the business today,
> but it also needs to be a strategic asset that could very much help the busi-
> ness tomorrow. It's all about a partnership between IT and the business. And
> given the right partnership, what you have is, if you like, a very strong future
> business strategy underwritten by a very good enabling IT strategy.

At Scottish Power, perhaps the best illustration of this idea grew out of the brilliant notion that a power company needn't be limited to selling power.

> I think that all industries, but especially utility industries, have to recognize
> that if they're going to succeed in the future world, they have got to
> broaden and widen their vision beyond what we would call the typical utility
> mindset.
>
> During '98 and early '99 I was promoting what the technology could do
> in addressing some of the major opportunities that the board was becoming
> aware of, especially in the consumer market. About twelve months before, I
> had started presenting a vision of how you answered the threats but also
> took advantage of the opportunities of e-commerce. So once the board real-
> ized they needed to do this, I became the logical person to initiate the effort
> and get it going.

Clearly the company wasn't planning to sell power over the Internet. So what does it mean for a utility move into e-com-merce? David Jones's explanation highlights the way he has helped show Scottish Power how to use technology to create new opportunities.

> *We don't necessarily have to offer our customers just electricity. We've got a good relationship with the customer, we've got a brand that is trusted, and we believe we can bring new process mindsets. If we go into an alliance with a bank, for example, we can offer financial services—which is what we have done in the last six months. We could offer both the bank and the customer new ways of working.*
>
> *This has everything to do with breaking out of a utility mindset.*

There would seem to be some risks, though, in an organization trying to do things that are not what it has historically done. How does a company take on the challenge of an e-commerce effort that represents a radical departure from what it knows how to do well, without stubbing its toe? How did they see that challenge at Scottish Power?

> *We can break our businesses down to two logical parts—the making of electricity, and the distribution and transmission of power across large areas of land to businesses and consumers.*
>
> *But when it comes to consumers, I think we've got a very simple choice. We could get out of the consumer game, and if we stay just supplying electricity, that's exactly what will happen to us. Or if we want to stay in the consumer game, we have to widen the portfolio of products and services that we offer to the consumer. It's either get out, or play the game entirely different. I didn't think we had any choice.*
>
> *Some of the utilities have the mindset that products and services and customer relationship are the same thing, run by the same operating division. That won't work in the future, it really won't work.*
>
> *One of the things we've had to grapple with and understand is that having a relationship with the customer has nothing to do with the products and services you offer. The Yahoos, the MSNs, the AOLs of this world are saying, To hell with the products and services, we will have the customer relation-*

ship, and we'll have a product service set covering every aspect of a consumer's lifestyle.

Yahoo—at least over here [in Europe] is saying, We will corral the players that provide the products and services. We'll corral the banks, we'll get the best deal for the consumer, and we'll handle the customer relationship for the bank, which becomes a pure product and service provider.

The play, of course, is that every provider will have to extend its line of products and services, and grow the customer relationship. You have to say, "We will develop this relationship by offering products and services that provide best value to the customer, from anywhere we can get them." And the company have to say to the business-unit managers, "You will create products and services, and take them to any market you like, but they must be guaranteed to be of best value to the customer."

It's this different mindset that's required when moving into e-commerce, which is the future of consumer marketing.

"E-commerce . . . is the future of consumer marketing." I couldn't agree more.

And an effective e-commerce solution must meet the same standard as any other business planning today: it must start from merging technology planning and business planning into a single, cohesive effort, driven by the business goals of the company.

*The Web will change relationships with
  employees.
We will never again have discussions where
  knowledge is hidden in somebody's pocket.
You will have to lead with ideas, not by
  controlling information.*

— JACK WELCH

What Workers Can See
and What Workers Can Say
Defines Their Importance

The idea is so familiar by now that it's almost boring to speak about: taking down the barriers that have traditionally kept most workers from access to most information. "Open-book management" has been the subject of books and *Harvard Business Review* articles since at least 1996.

But like a lot of other good management ideas, this one has been honored with great word of mouth and a great deal less action. The reasons, though, are not hard to figure. Leading the list: It's been true probably since the dawn of human society that those with more information held greater power—the clan leader, tribal chief, medicine woman. And the child tapped to become apprentice to the medicine woman, taught the mysteries kept hidden from the rest, would gain power from the secret knowledge.

The king leading his troops into battle shared his plans for the engagement with his noblemen and commanders but not with the foot soldiers, archers, and horsemen who would do most of the fighting. The feudal lord might have himself been barely literate, but still knew more of the nation and the neighboring villages than did his peasants. From the time of the Industrial Revolution, the workers running the machines were told what to do, when, and how, but it would have occurred to no one to tell them why.

In the modern company it's been a truism forever that the production-floor manager and the head of the typing pool had a lot of information denied to those who worked under them. They in turn were denied access to, and likely saw no reason they should have, other information that the higher-level managers and the executives used for making their decisions.

You know how this scenario plays—you likely see it in action every day of your working life: the higher you rise in the organization, the more of the privileged "inside" information you gain access to. In fact, how much of the key information you're permitted to look at is a leading measure of your importance and power in the pecking order.

Nothing new in all of that. What's new is this idea that the organization will function better and be more successful if you share information more widely, presenting employees with an "open book" to find out whatever they want or need about the company's structure, operations, and plans.

One of the essentials that makes today's fourth era of computing so unique, unlike anything we've seen before, is the element of connectivity—the desktop computer (or laptop) plus the Internet (or the in-company version, the Intranet) equals the ability to be connected to anybody, anywhere, at any time of the day or night.

So the restrictions on access that a company puts on anyone in the organization means that person is limited in how the technology can pay off for them. I love how people in organizations, all of us, sometimes say one thing but do another. We say employees are our most important asset, but we keep lids clamped on the information, treating much of the company knowledge as if it were national security data.

Yes, it does seem logical to demand, Why should Mary Jane, who's a secretary in Product Development, want to look at the P&L of our business operations in Chile? Most organizations put restrictions on that, wondering what on earth use she could make of the information.

Surprise: At Microsoft, Mary Jane is allowed, with a minimum of exceptions, to see virtually any company information she wants. The presumption is that she must have some good reason for wanting to look. Maybe nothing will come of it, or maybe it was just idle curiosity or time wasting. On the other hand, maybe she'll suggest this brilliant idea about something we can do better. But she doesn't have to prove a need to know before accessing the data, doesn't need anyone's permission, doesn't have to worry that someone will call her on the carpet for it.

Certainly there's some information that's not available to every employee. The financial numbers are kept close to the vest until the official quarterly announcement; like every other public company, we'd be in hot water with the SEC if we didn't. Certain other things, like advanced product plans, are also obviously too sensitive to share.

But most organizations waste effort thinking about what information their employees *shouldn't* have . . . and lose the benefits they could gain from breaking down the information barriers.

These days the Internet brings a whole new meaning to the word "information." Yet, now that it seems access to virtually everything workers might ever want to know to do their jobs better has been brought to their desktops, what are the world's businesses doing to benefit from it?

I'm dumbfounded to visit company after company where employees have to fill out a form and submit it to some newly created department, the function of which is to decide that Thou shalt be granted access to the Internet, or Thou shalt not. I'm sure these companies believe they're being open with their employees, but they act as if the workers are either not trustworthy enough or not smart enough to derive any benefit from the Internet.

Some companies try to elevate the level of their professional staff by terming them "knowledge workers," a label I dislike because it implies there are other workers in the organization who *don't* have a need for knowledge. That, to me, is ridiculous, a bizarre concept left over from the dark ages of business—laughable, if it weren't for the damage it does to the company and to those individuals who are by implication classified as mindless automatons.

Sometimes we fail to recognize powerful solutions even when they're right in front of our noses. The CEO of a major retailing firm in Australia, recounted an experience from earlier in his career that taught him an unforgettable lesson.

Dennis Eck:

I was involved with a large, successful retail chain, but they had thirteen stores that were losing something like two and a half million a year. They were considered to be so bad, the management figured that no idea would make them any worse.

So they decided to break them off into a separate unit and give them over to this small group of people. Very small—me, and one other person, and a secretary. I said to the person I was working with, "Why don't we go into this room here and figure out what to do before we start?" Which sounds trite, but can you imagine how many companies have made mistakes by actually doing something before they thought about what to do?

So we sat there and we thought, and thought and thought, and in a couple of weeks, we had a list that looked like a thousand things to do up on the board—obviously thirteen stores that are losing that much money have many things wrong with them.

I said, "You know, I think we can't get anywhere until we decide what's the one thing to do." He looked at me and said, "Dennis, that's impossible, there are a thousand things we need to do." I said, "Why don' t we sit here until we can figure out the one thing that we want to start with."

Finally we agreed on one thing we would try to change: people in a losing business understand they' re losers; we had to convince them they could win.

The plan was that we would distribute information to them, and then let them make the decisions. And the hope was that in making their own decisions, they would build their confidence, begin making right decisions, and that would create an environment of winning. So rather than sending them their product prices, and what their retails were, we went out and sat down with them and said, "These are what your costs are this week and we need a 35 percent gross margin. How do you think you can do that?"

This was even riskier than it sounds. Dennis Eck describes the staff as "people who had matriculated down to the lowest earning stores because they were considered not to be very good, and had actually been demoted."

The store people would do their price lists and we' d say, "That' s fine, and you agree to this margin and this level of sales. Anything you do within reason to get that, please do—but remember you' re on the line for these two things."

After about a year and a half, with no refurbishment, those stores went from losing, to breaking even, and at the end of another year they were actually making about a million dollars.

And the key, the independent variable, is to encourage people to engage their brains at the door.

But the story actually does not have a happy ending.

The stores became successful enough that they could be brought back into the mainstream business. But that meant that instructions were distributed to the people and they executed them, as opposed to information distributed and they decided what to do.

All thirteen of those stores became unprofitable again.

I consider this a powerful example of the value of giving people access to information, and then letting them make the most of it.

Maybe it's obvious or maybe it's not, but one essential in this whole issue of the value of information revolves around whom you permit to have an e-mail address. It's the key that unlocks access to company information and bestows the ability for workers to have a say about company business.

Clearly a worker needs an e-mail address for sending messages and receiving them, but she also needs an address simply for signing on to the Intranet and the Internet.

The e-mail address works both ways, of course: Beyond opening the gates to information and communication, it gives the company the protection of knowing who accesses what information, and who sent what e-mail. Unless you have a highly skilled hacker on your staff, there's no such thing as an e-mail equivalent to anonymous hate mail or harassing phone calls.

If someone at Microsoft I don't know sends me an e-mail, I can almost instantly find out what their title is, what their phone number is, who they work for, who works for them. Anybody who takes part in a company debate does so openly—in full view, so to speak. If you launch a scurrilous attack, you do it fully aware that everyone who reads the messages knows you're the one who sent them . . . which tends to keep a debate on a somewhat more even keel.

I can't swear to you about this research because I got it secondhand, but I've heard in speeches a comment about how 3M did a study in 1990 and determined that their people were working on collaborative efforts something like 10 to 15 percent of the time. And now in the year 2000, they've determined it's something like 40 to 50 percent. And a full 25 percent of the participants in the collaborative work are in locations remote from one another.

Part of that is the changing nature of the economy, but part of it is the changing way in which technology allows people to work together. That's one example of a barrier coming down.

So the importance of someone in the organization is in part defined by how much access to information the company grants the person; that's the "What you can *see*" part. Another large part of this: how much leeway the person has to express their thoughts and ideas. This is the "What you can *say*" part.

One European bank I visited several years ago had a separate little elevator for the executive wing. At that time, for visitors in the waiting room—I swear this is true—they ironed the newspaper and presented it to you warm with your tea, until a stuffy aide came and whispered that the muckety-muck you were waiting for could see you. Any company that has a culture like this, you can just imagine the result if some junior loan officer at a branch in the town of Creamcheese-on-Bagel, fired with a brilliant idea for improving service to customers, tried to e-mail his suggestion directly to the bank's chairman.

I remember at one presentation I did, some of the people present got quite passionate about the suggestion of opening the information vaults to everyone. The CEO of one company assured me with some heat that this would just never work in their culture. The idea that clerical people, for example, would have access to basic information on the financial status of the company, even if it were public information, was so contrary to their culture that it would simply not be acceptable. This is not rocket science, people; the potential benefits should be obvious.

Okay, sure—I don't expect every company in every country to shift overnight to a completely open environment. But the world is

changing. Even that stuffy European bank with the private executive elevator and the steam-pressed newspapers has grown a lot less
stuffy since I first visited there, perhaps in part because they've
brought in hordes of people from outside the banking culture.

There's a lesson in this story.

If you think about the traditional corporate structure, what deter-
mines who's going to be a part of a debate? Simple: the people who
are allowed in the meeting room.

In the Microsoft corporate structure, much of the debating is vir-
tual because of electronic mail; it is not sectioned off to a single
physical room. This obviously gives much greater, much broader
participation. And the culture says that anybody can join in any
debate on any subject.

If my administrative assistant, for example, wants to send a note
to the chairman, she can do it—doesn't have to check with me,
doesn't have to cc forty-seven people and have a committee meeting
to decide how the thing should be worded. She just sends it. And
she can expect a response signed "Bill G," probably within twenty-
four hours.

Or if she wants to get involved in a debate about how to market
Word 2000 in Bolivia or what features Excel should have in
Indonesia, she can. The view is that everyone in the company has
that right. If they have something of value to add, excellent; if
they're wasting people's time, they better be prepared to get yelled
at. They know the risk. Why hold anybody back?

Just because people wherever I go always seem curious about the
workings of Microsoft, I want to lift the curtain and describe a little
about how the place functions.

In many traditional companies, you find the familiar suggestion
boxes—you write up a suggestion and drop it in the box, and some

probably anonymous committee considers it, and maybe you end up getting a gift of a night out on the town with your spouse.

I'm sure lots of good examples of ideas came from suggestion boxes. At Microsoft, we take this idea one giant step further.

The permission we grant to share views with the head of the company has come into sharpest focus when we've faced one of those chasms that require a challenging leap into the unknown. The most widely written-about chasm in recent times for us was one you've likely heard about—Microsoft getting religion about the Internet, and playing catch-up. It's a subject that would make a book in itself. A few snippets bear on the point at hand.

The Microsoft/Internet story began to hit the front pages in the mid-1990s when two of the key Wall Street analysts covering the company downgraded the stock because, they said, we had missed the Internet, that technology had taken a jog and Microsoft hadn't noticed, and was now charging headlong in an old direction while the leaders in the new industry were building impenetrable fortresses.

In fact, conversations had already been going on inside Microsoft for some time about the Internet. With the phenomenal success of browser software that now smoothed the process of finding your way through the maze, even for a novice, the debate had heated up quickly. Lots of Microsoft people thought the phenomenon was real and the face of the future, and that we were not moving fast enough.

The Microsoft culture is in part a not-always-polite debating society. Everybody is permitted to voice their views; I'd almost say that everybody is *expected* to. Not only do we not have a set of rules about how you may communicate and who you may send messages to, we actually encourage a degree of anarchy in speaking out. If you have a point of view that's different from the accepted, you're expected to take on the hierarchy of the company and share your thinking. (On the other hand, everyone understands that it's okay to have a hard-core discussion about ideas, but not okay to fire off personal attacks against the people who disagree.)

Because we have just one standard way to communicate—a single, unified e-mail system available twenty-four hours a day, seven days a week—everyone can easily participate wherever on earth they are, no matter the country, no matter the time zone, no matter their position in the company. At times like this the Microsoft in-your-face culture produces a highly charged atmosphere in which junior workers electronically bombard people several layers higher in the organization with facts, suggestions, and opinions.

That's exactly what happened in the Internet debate. Many fairly junior people, even people new to the company, fairly fresh off the college campus, decided that some of the fairly senior people weren't getting the message about how fundamental the Internet was going to become to the whole structure of communication and commerce. Some of the more compelling arguments came from these youngsters. Which isn't surprising; if you think about those days, in the mid-nineties, it was on the college campuses that the Internet had heated up and turned into something more than an esoteric tool for the specialist. So the young crowd at Microsoft came to this internal debate with a lot more passion, because they had actually used the Internet and so had a better vision of its potential. To them it was like skateboarders trying to sell the idea of the skateboard to executives who had grown rich manufacturing nothing but Barbie dolls.

Microsoft's sales VP remembers this vividly.

Jeff Raikes:
The way in which Jay Allard and others rose up and said, "Hey, you know, we're not focused on the Internet the way we need to be" was stirring things up. This was back in 1994 and was primarily an e-mail debate.

Meanwhile, lots of Microsoft people thought it didn't make good sense to slow down other programs and throw a massive effort into designing Internet solutions. So that was the debate—some sure we had to make a decision very quickly, others just as sure time was on our side and we'd be making a terrible mistake to move in too much of a hurry.

> You can argue that in a corporation where they didn't have that kind of free flow of information, the issue would never even really have bubbled up. Would a guy four levels down in the organization have gotten the meeting with the CEO, as Jay Allard did? But in our case, Bill Gates was getting the e-mail and he was reading it.

The Internet debate turned into a battle of the bits about what the Internet meant and what we should do to deal with it, with tons of e-mail flying back and forth every day. And a lot of it wasn't composed with an emphasis on tact. Not the standard tone of communications in your own organization, I'm sure.

Around here you have to be okay with debates in which you get no respect from people just because you have something like "senior vice president" in your title. People who disagree with you can, as in my examples, be intemperate in their language. (In our interviewing process, we try to give people a sense of what the culture is like, and screen out those whose natures would make them uncomfortable when the sleet hits the fan and push comes to shove.)

In the Internet debate, the younger advocates, in particular, kept up a barrage, they kept pounding their points. And they'd get responses from executives who didn't see matters the same way, who were pushing back, pushing back, pushing back.

As that debate went on internally, it caused some minds to change at the top. When Microsoft executives began after a few months to think that maybe, Yes, the Internet was looking like it was going to be huge and, Yes, it was definitely happening a hell of a lot faster than we anticipated, the company then began to review what would have to change, and what it would mean from a product development perspective, and what it would mean from a sales and marketing perspective.

The debate continued with increasing intensity until the late summer of 1995, when an e-mail went out to all employees. In one instant, everywhere on earth, everybody in the company got the same message, which said in the header: From billg.

When a message comes in from Bill G, you read it before doing anything else. In some detail the message laid out what path we were going to follow, how we would do it, the implications for every part of the company.

At that time of year, our annual planning cycle had ended and the new business year had recently begun. Nobody was about to point that out. The decision had been made. The company was going to change, starting right then—no more studies, no more debates, no more uncertainty, just do it now and do it quick.

There's that Microsoft culture at work again—the democracy transforming in a blink, the incredibly swift shift from everybody participating in the debate to everybody having the discipline to turn the big ship quickly.

On December 7 of that year (I've always wondered but never asked if Bill Gates chose the date to give some kind of message), the announcement of our new strategy and direction was made to the world, and the company demonstrated twenty new Internet-related products. *Twenty.*

And that's how, in less than six months, we already had products to show—especially important in the very visible and pivotal browser space.

As a sidelight on this—and here I'm pulling aside the curtain again—an issue that comes up from time to time, especially during debates like the one over our participation in the Internet, concerns whether the company will give rewards to people who suggest important ideas that become the basis for a new product, solve some business problem, or otherwise contribute to revenues or to saving money.

We have a simple answer when people raise this question: "No."

At Microsoft we don't give awards for suggestions, we don't often give rewards when an employee suggests a job candidate who eventually gets hired. Some years ago there was a debate over this and the question landed on Bill Gates's desk. In essence his reply was, Absolutely not. He said, "If you don't think it's your responsibility to make sure that the best people work at Microsoft, I don't want you here."

And so rather than having an electronic suggestion box or a new hire bonus program, we basically say, That's everyone's responsibility; we respect you enough as an employee to give you access to sacred things and trust you to deal with them properly. In return, we expect you to share your suggestions and to give us the names of likely job candidates. Information should be a two-way street. The rewards are indirect: We all share as stockholders in the success of the company, and people who make special contributions of course are recognized when it comes time for bonuses, salary increases, and promotions.

I was in New Orleans early in 2000 giving a speech to a few thousand folks from partner companies that deliver training in Microsoft products. The people in the audience listened to my views on opening the gates of information and communication to everyone in the company, and gave me a standing ovation.

Nice for the ego, but I know from experience that many of those folks went back home, went into the office on Monday morning and did *nothing* to change the practices at their companies.

Listen to me: This is a classic Dilbert thing going on here. Classic.

Unless you're prepared to open the floodgates to constructive criticism and debate from *all* levels, independent of rank, your company will not be able to stay competitive in the Digital Age. (Unless, I suppose, you're in an industry so backward that none of your competitors get it, either—not your competitors in the United States, nor the competitors you have or soon will have from around the globe.)

The real challenge here isn't technical, it's only political. The technical part is easy. Installing a uniform, company-wide messaging infrastructure and giving people the access I'm talking about is a relatively trivial technical task.

Two issues: Can your senior executive group adjust to a culture in which folks at the most junior levels of the organization have access to all but the most highly sensitive information about the company? And can they adjust to a culture in which they will receive e-mails from those same junior-level folks? Will they be open and responsive to those e-mails? Are the managers at levels between the junior sender and the executive who receives the e-mail going to revolt at not being consulted before the message gets sent, probably not even being cc'ed?

Again, I'm not arguing for anarchy. Everybody needs to understand you don't send junk mail or abusive messages to the chairman or CEO—or anybody else, for that matter. On the other hand, there needs to be some understanding as well on the part of the company, that it won't work to write a set of restrictive Do's and Don'ts: People will avoid being stupid about this because you hired sensible people in the first place.

It's remarkable what a change to this kind of open environment can do to fire up a spirit of "We're all in this together" at virtually any company.

No businessperson is, literally, more than six-
tenths of a second
away from any other businessperson.
When I need a partner, I can just as easily look
in Bangalore, India, as next door in my
Silicon Valley neighborhood.

—Tom Peters

A New Weapon:
Strategic Partners

"Would you like to put some of your R&D people together with ours, and let them jointly work on finding the best solutions for your needs?"

Ten years ago, I can't imagine many companies asking a question like that of their suppliers. Today, it's happening more and more often.

But not often enough. In too many companies, the vendor relationship is still based on RFPs and RFIs and beating up suppliers for the cheapest price. Maybe a request for proposals is justified for buying pencils and copier toner cartridges and photographic supplies. It makes no sense at all for buying technology.

By the same token, it's time technology suppliers stopped treating customers as a quota. That means no more overselling the products and underselling the weakness of their offering. It means no more hiding the need for services and support. Technology companies (including Microsoft, I hasten to add) have an obligation to define what service and support has to be included with a sale in order to ensure a successful user experience, and advise the customer so they can buy the appropriate levels as part of the contract.

At Microsoft, we took that a giant step further. If we have a customer in the insurance business, for example, we might say, "We'd like to offer you the opportunity of working with our voice-recognition people on how you could automate the process of collecting information from policyholders calling to file claims."

Fine—but what I'm talking about goes beyond any sort of one-time arrangement you offer as an inducement to closing a sale. What I'm talking about is—

Turning vendors into strategic partners.

At Microsoft we have a long-held practice of depending on outside companies to provide a lot of the service on our products. We have our own consulting group, we have our own product support group, and so on, but we have thousands of outside partners as well that provide services for us. Everybody from Anderson Consulting to little mom-and-pop operations. For several years, we—just like most of our competitors—held technical briefings on upcoming new products that are given in two separate categories of sessions: one series for the partners (only those who had signed Non-Disclosure Agreements, of course, of course) and another series for our employees.

For the employee sessions, briefers who came from the product group to present their story were assured in advance that all those in the audience would be Microsoft people, so they could tell the entire story. For the other sessions, the speakers were cautioned that they'd be speaking to "outsiders," and they'd be given guidelines about what they would be allowed to say and what they'd have to avoid.

Many years ago, we decided to do things differently, starting with our annual technical training session for field people. We began including a sampling of Microsoft partners in the same audience. It was almost funny watching the presenters react to this. "I've got things I need to say to the other technical employees and the sales and support people that I can't tell the outsiders. Now, how do I do this?"

Classic Ballmer. He said, "Well, why *wouldn't* you tell them everything?"

"They're not Microsoft people, we can't tell them everything."

"Now wait a minute," Steve said. "You're telling me we're going to send Microsoft people out with full knowledge, the good, the bad, and the ugly, about the new products, so when they go on-site to help the customer, they know everything. But these partners of ours, whose job is to go out and do the same thing with customers for us, we're basically going to shortchange them, and tell them only part of the story. And then they'll go on-site to help the customer and screw it up, or give bad information. And our product will be blamed for it."

The people who attended the technical briefing that year, *all* of them, got the same picture about the products. And it's been that way ever since.

Out of that change we gained new respect from our partners. When they saw they were being treated equally, treated truly as partners, the impact was giant.

One of the worst things that can happen to any company is overselling yourself. You want your stuff to be used only where it's going to work, and if it doesn't work, you want everybody to know how to fix it.

I've always thought that the Microsoft experience was a first-class example of learning to treat those you do business with like true partners.

We've traditionally extended this idea of treating others as partners to additional areas of how we relate to the outside world—in particular, with customers. How far do we go in practice about being open with them? One example: We run customer visits every day at our large Briefing Center. I often speak to these groups, and so do other Microsoft executives. One of the things that we try to do for all of our customers on their first visit is to take them through our own internal MIS organization. And we have them meet with, not sales and marketing people, but MIS staff, who tell them, Here's how we run this software you're interested in, here are shortcuts we've learned, here are some things we've had to build because of inadequacies in the software, here are the mistakes we've made that, boy, we wish somebody could have told us about.

They're giving the customers a real sense of what it takes to manage our MIS complex and to run the software. Nobody ever tells our MIS people, Don't talk about this, Don't mention that, Don't give a straight answer if they ask about thus and so. Moreover, the MIS people know that nobody's looking over their shoulders to listen in and censor what they're saying.

That buys us a zillion points; the feedback we get is gigantically positive. In fact, it's gone over so well that we now consider this part of the duties of the MIS department. Its core job obviously is to keep up the systems to run our company, but the tours have become such a credibility point with customers that we now make sure MIS has enough head count that it always has highly experienced people available to handle these visits—actual working MIS people, not newbies with limited knowledge hired just to show visitors around.

Typical of how we now relate to major customers is the close relationship we have with Lloyds TSB, the British banking firm; we have connections with them up and down the chain. I go over three times a year to meet with their executive staff, the CIO, and some of the business management people. And a group of top Lloyds TSB people comes over to Redmond every year.

These aren't sales meetings—they've already licensed our software. Instead, they may want to talk about new products or customer offerings they're rolling out and ask whether Microsoft has any solutions in the works that may bear on what they're doing. They might ask where we think wireless laptop communications is going. On one occasion they wanted to hear our views on what other financial institutions are doing about leveraging the Internet.

When Lloyds is evaluating a merger opportunity, we might be asked, Look, if we do this, what are the technology implications?

In effect, we're asking customers like this, How can we help you? We go to some lengths to give solid answers to their requests, even when the information we're giving is not going to sell any software or bring Microsoft any new revenue. These are executive-to-executive, high-level discussions—briefings and exchanges of information on a confidential level, in two directions.

My closest contact at Lloyds TSB is with Archie Kane, whom we introduced earlier in these pages. The way he came to his present position at the bank, and his role there, offer a vivid illustration of the rocky path a once stodgy organization has had to travel in order to remake itself for the e-business era.

Archie Kane:

The Information Technology group was virtually a company within a company, tightly guarded like a heavily walled castle. How it came to its decisions, how it dealt with its suppliers, and what it did in terms of the technology it was buying, implementing, and supplying was really kept a mystery to the rest of the organization.

I felt going forward that IT was so important, we had to get it out from behind the walls of the castle and more into the business arena.

For Lloyds TSB, "treating the supplier as a strategic partner" isn't a concept or a goal; it has become a practical, everyday working reality.

The first time a new prospective supplier comes in, we go through a strategic pitch: "This is what drives us, this is how we do shareholder value, this is how we calculate economic profit, this is how we do business cases. And here are the strategic issues that are currently on our Top Ten list; we're willing to go through any of these and discuss one by one any of them in depth where you think you can add value."

Then we say, "Go off and have a look, have a think. And the next time we meet, let's talk about two or three of these items that you think you can help us with."

But we also tell them very clearly, "Don't come back with, Oh boy, we can help you in every single one of these and here are ten different ways we can do it." That's just not realistic.

From the time we first started doing that, it went very well from the supplier end. To me, that's not surprising.

Another direction the bank has gone in turning its suppliers into strategic partners involves R&D and the highly uncertain technology future.

Archie Kane:

We had a technology research and development department. They ended up spending much of their time playing with a lot of new toys and gizmos.

We've basically dismantled that now. We really don't need to do that anymore because we can avail ourselves of key people at our supplier firms who are out there doing the advanced research. And if they're not doing work in some particular area, they know who's doing it and they can get us in to see those people.

So in effect we've shifted our R&D to our suppliers. They're a lot better at it than we were, better than we would probably ever be. The best we'd ever be able to do is second-guess what they were doing. When we partner with them—not just as a customer but as a true strategic partner—we can avail ourselves of all the work they're doing, all the labs, the technology, the

Ph.D.'s. And their research partners, as well—because the whole world is a world of partnering in technology now.

How does "turning suppliers into partners" translate into real-world actions?

Archie Kane:

Several years ago I became concerned that the main relationships with a number of our suppliers was at too low a level. They were being dealt with at a very technical level, which meant we were potentially missing out on some of the more strategic implications of technology.

To be fair, I didn't come at this problem purely from a technology point of view. I came at it from the point of view of who could be important strategic suppliers for Lloyds TSB—who would we want to engage in more of a strategic partnership, whereby we share some of our confidential strategic thinking, and in turn they engage in a reciprocal sort of arrangement?

One area where this made sense was telecommunications, which is absolutely crucial for us, as it is for most financial services companies. We had a number of contracts with telecom suppliers and some of those relationships were not particularly well organized, in terms of what we did in-house and what we had the suppliers doing under contract.

Kane led a rethinking of these relationships, bringing about a dramatic reduction in the number of firms that the Information Technology group of Lloyds TSB was dealing with. And he changed the nature of the relationship with those firms kept in the fold from a tactical level to a strategic one, by dealing himself directly with high-level executives of the other firms.

There were a number of approaches I took. One of them was that I wanted to raise key suppliers to a higher level where we would meet on a regular basis, once every three or four months, and exchange an understanding of each other's business. We had never engaged suppliers on that basis.

I wanted to deal with very senior people at those supplier companies, and have them deal with senior people on our side, and together we would create this strategic platform.

And that's basically how we came to the idea of establishing our Strategic Supplier Forum. When we identified the key companies we wanted to include in such a Forum, they came down to IT and telecom companies. Because if you look at what banks buy, after payroll and property, the biggest things are IT and telecom.

I was honored when Lloyds TSB invited Microsoft to be included as a vendor in their Supplier Forum, and it's been enlightening for me personally to work with them and see how the forum operates.

By raising the level of the relationships, we started to get a very good picture of where the key dependencies were. And also, we began to get a much better picture of the sort of problems we were facing.

But the path to progress is rarely smooth. The very first time Kane and his people tried to select a single supplier and use the forum approach, they ran into unexpected problems.

The supplier we chose had never done that kind of project in the U.K. before, and they had to go through a very steep learning curve. And it was the biggest IT contract of its kind in the U.K. at that time.

Things did not go smoothly or sweetly. We went through very, very difficult times in the rollout, very difficult relations with the supplier, to the point of renegotiating the deal.

But if we hadn't had the Strategic Supplier Forum and a strategic supplier relationship, when the project hit rough times, we would almost certainly have ended up disengaging, we would have canceled the contract and brought in the lawyers. And that would have been a grave upset—it would have been a failure that set us back months, perhaps even a year or more.

As it was, once the matter had escalated to the Strategic Supplier Forum, it was constantly on the agenda whenever we met, over a period of about nine months as we struggled through that really difficult period. The supplier had their top people on it from the States, and I was actively engaged in monitoring. So the thing had a spotlight on it from the highest levels on both sides.

Not that it was easy, but in the end we got through the problems, and we're now successfully rolling out the program.

The main lesson we learned from that experience was that we had not spent sufficient time in defining our requirements up front. When you embark on the type of effort where you're breaking new ground, and have to go through a learning phase with a supplier, a strategic relationship can make all the difference.

"Forum" sounds like a group that gathers regularly for face-to-face meetings. In fact, the operation is quite different.

The supplier firms that are members of the forum don't all come here and sit down together; rather, we get together with them independently. But a number of them know that some of their competitors are also members of the forum. What they will sometimes do is to get together to collaborate on a particular solution that they know we will need. IBM, for example, may work with Oracle or another firm to get our particular solutions going.

If a business unit of Lloyds TSB has a particular issue or area that's of great interest to them, then their leader can come along when we have forum sessions with a supplier that might be able to offer a solution. And that happens on frequent occasions.

Now we're currently looking at whether we should move one or two other areas onto the Strategic Supplier Forum—for example, the logistics companies we deal with.

Another success of the forum approach involved one of Lloyds TSB's worldwide IT supplier firms.

We heard from the local chief executive of one of our South American operations that he and his team were having IT problems. Their IT was outsourced under contract to one of the major global firms, which was outsourcing the work to yet another firm. So there was a triangular relationship that was making it even harder to push for resolution, and the mess was going from bad to worse.

Our chief executive in that country called and asked me to address the issue with the forum contact at our supplier firm. I worked out an arrangement where the worldwide account director of the other firm would visit that country to see what he could do. He went over there within a week, solved the problem, and got people to cooperate—because he had the authority to do it.

This important issue was cleared up rather easily, and it's an example of how the forum concept can be used at a business-unit level.

From the time I first heard about it to the day it was resolved was probably about two months. Whereas in the past, problems like that would rattle around for a very long time.

The idea of establishing strategic relationships can—*should*—work in both directions.

Archie Kane:

If you have a supplier who sees a strategic relationship as just an opportunity to deal with people at a high level in your company, a wedge to sell you more goods, the idea really doesn't work very well. And I have to say we've had one or two who tried that. We had to drop one supplier because of it.

One of the great benefits we've reaped has been that in return, some suppliers have invited us in to look at how they run their company. How do they organize themselves? How do they develop strategy? How do they do their financial control? How do they do the strategic planning? How do they do their MIS? How do they equip their people? How do they develop their own competencies? That's been a fantastic insight for us.

So the arrangement works best when you have a supplier who sees an opportunity to operate in a different manner. The suppliers who I think have gained the most from the strategic relationship with us are those suppliers who actively engage and then invite us to share in some of their thinking.

What makes that so valuable is, I believe, because it will become part of the solution as corporations evolve at an ever more rapid rate, as we move into the new, e-business type of world. Businesses that have been around for decades or a hundred years and have evolved at a certain leisurely pace now have to try new ways of doing things.

At Lloyds TSB, we're continually looking for insight into how leading companies are doing that, which gives us fantastic insight into how we can deploy some of those operational models into our own business.

Bottom line: Archie Kane has no doubts about the value of strategic relationships in strengthening the effectiveness of an IT organization in meeting the needs of the company it serves.

Archie Kane:

Today I can sift through very quickly and identify the really rich veins that we could pursue with suppliers. Before we instigated the forum, this was very much on an ad hoc basis—individuals going on trips, attending conferences, learning from consultants. Those are all a much more desperate way of doing, of trying to stay ahead of the learning curve.

Perhaps most important of all, the level of learning about IT and technology at the most senior levels of the company is much greater than it used to be. We reap the benefits of that virtually every day.

CHAPTER 8

*The big won't beat the small;
the fast will beat the slow.*

—JOHN CHAMBERS, Cisco

The New Power of
Alliances and "Coopetition"

When we think about strategic alliances, we tend to think of established, proven companies smart enough to be looking for operating advantages or expanded business opportunities.

But a striking development has been taking place among today's start-ups. Especially in Silicon Valley and the myriad Silicon Valley–wannabe communities around the United States, young companies have been discovering that strategic alliances can offer a fast track to becoming established and recognized.

In many ways these hyperpaced, high-energy start-ups are writing the book on establishing alliances and making them pay off in quick time. Others take note: Whatever the size of your organization, whatever industry you're in, a new pattern is being set that you can ill afford to ignore. I'm convinced it's a pattern that will become an essential for companies that intend to stay in the game.

Here's one example of how this new adventure is being played. From a base in the high-tech heaven of northern California, the Internet start-up FreeSamples.com aims to give consumers an opportunity to "try before you buy," while giving merchandisers a way of distributing product samples only to consumers who specifically request them (which sounds like a big improvement over coming home and finding that a sample of denture paste has been left dangling from your doorknob).

Jeff Malkin, the co-founder and CEO of FreeSamples, shared his experiences in the mostly unexplored arena of start-ups seeking to form strategic alliances.

Jeff Malkin:

> When I finished my business plan, the very first action I took was contacting the major portals to try to talk about creating a strategic alliance—for a company that wasn't even launched yet, didn't even have a Web site yet. I had firsthand knowledge, from friends and from things I was reading, about how a company can just be made because of the right alliances.
>
> A friend of mine had shared an idea with me about When.com, a company he and his partners had been developing. After two rounds of funding and $7.5 million raised, they sold the company to AOL for about $150 million—in fourteen months! And it was at that point I decided to focus full time not only on FreeSamples.com but on forming these very important strategic relationships.

One key that unlocks many doors for an Internet start-up is establishing a relationship with one of the major portals. These are Web sites designed to be used as a visitor's gateway onto the Internet; think of Microsoft Network, Yahoo or Excite—each offering a wide variety of options available at a click, such as news and sports results, stock market info, weather, travel planning, chat rooms, and much more. The leading portals, because they enjoy millions of visitors a day, have established a commanding presence on the Web.

While trying to make headway with the portals, Jeff was also focusing on other kinds of strategic relationships. The first one to fall into place was with a major national product distribution firm.

The relationship was twofold. On one side of the equation they were going to be our distribution firm, and on the other side they were going to be representing us as an outsource sales channel to all their existing consumer-product customers.

With that relationship, I would be able to close my angel round of financing, $1.8 million. I vividly remember the lead investor telling me straight out, "Unless you can close that distribution deal, I'm not going to put in my money."

At that point I was stuck in a "chicken or egg, which comes first?" scenario: The portals that were interested were not going to sign anything until I had the angel round closed. The angel money wasn't going to close until I had my distribution firm in place. The distribution firm didn't want to close unless I had some brand managers of major products signed up to let us distribute their samples. And the brands weren't going to close unless I had one or two major portals signed up.

It was a wide circle that I kept bringing closer and closer. I had to try to convince one of them to fall.

When you're trying to come out of the gate before an angel round, a letter of intent can mean everything. I said to the distribution firm, "We've got these guys over here who are ready to sign as long as you close this." I asked them to give me a letter of intent that basically said if I could deliver two national brands, they would become my distribution partner. And finally, they did. It was the missing link, a piece of gold.

That's what allowed us to close the angel round. And the money from the angel investors then allowed me to attract some very good talent to my management team. That talent allowed me to form the next big relationship with the next company, and so on and so on. It all starts with getting that very first deal in place.

Jeff soon realized that not all strategic alliances are equal.

An interesting thing I've discovered over the last year is that there are groups of partnerships. They can really make a start-up that can figure out how to take advantage of them.

You begin to notice as you talk with different companies and start to form alliances that there are what I call separate "circles." If Lycos is partnered with company A and company B, then Excite will partner with company C and company D that are competitive with A and B. And I started to notice that the central companies and the peripheral ones were basically getting closer and closer until the central company would acquire the others.

So I began to see the necessity of being part of these rings or end up being excluded. And it was more out of the fear of being excluded than the actual desire to be partnering with some of these companies that led me to try to form relationships.

What would have happened if we had been excluded? It would have meant having no portal deals at all. No portal deals would have meant not having the ability to erect any really significant barriers to keep a competitor from coming in and just stepping up and taking over our space—offering the same solution that we offer.

(The word "space" has come to have a special meaning in the argot of high-tech communities. "What space are you in?" a venture capitalist might ask, meaning, What particular, narrowly defined industry segment are you going after? FreeSamples defines its space as marketing promotion, or market research.)

These rings set up a barrier against your competitors, because there's only room for one type of company in each ring. If you're the one, then your competitors are excluded.

Even among leading portals, Jeff believes, there's a hierarchy.

The goal really is to get into the AOL ring—to start climbing up these different rings until AOL finally notices you and decides they have to have you in their family.

Or there's another possible course. When you become sufficiently noticed, Internet capital firms like CMGI and Safeguard, that are constantly investing in companies, may add you to their network.

Again, they won't add two online product sampling market research com-
panies like FreeSamples.com, they'll add only one. If you're that one, then
you have all the positive effects of being a part of their network—whether
it's helping to raise money, whether it's bringing in clients, whether it's just
having the CMGI or the Safeguard name behind you. On the Web, being part
of a network is a necessity.

And especially important if you're establishing a new niche, as FreeSam-
ples is doing.

But hoping to join forces with a strategic partner that's umpteen
times your size brings its own challenge. The difficult question:
When do you start letting people know what you're doing? If you
begin telling your story too early, an AOL or somebody may say,
What a great idea—and then put some software engineers on doing
it and capturing the space before you do.

It's a very interesting conflict. I'm working with some other start-ups that
are coming out of the gates and that question comes up a lot. And my first
answer is usually, Look, if you don't talk about it, no one's going to know
who you are, and if your company is young enough where you really have
nothing, then you've got nothing to lose. If you stay in the stealth mode,
nobody's going to hear about you.

Right now, with our second round of financing in place, we're still staying
in stealth mode to the public until we launch the Web site.

(The FreeSamples.com site went online for Beta testing about
two months after this interview, in June 2000.)

But you have to be out there forming these relationships and the only way to
do it is to spread the word about what you're doing.

The building of a company proceeds in baby steps. Once you get one
partner on board, once you build one relationship with a big company, then
the next ones are easier to get. And once you get those, the ones after that

are easier still. And then eventually people are coming to you and knocking down your door.

At FreeSamples, we're on that borderline right now where people are actually starting to come to us to partner. The hardest one is that very first one.

If anything gives testimony to the rapid pace of business in this e-business age, it's the speed with which companies like FreeSamples conclude deals and become revenue-generating organizations.

Right now, closing the second round of financing, for $15 million, I'd say we are right on the brink of exploding out of the gates. We already have major relationships with several of the leading portals and with sixty-five brands, including most of the top consumer package manufacturers like Procter and Gamble, Unilever, Kelloggs, and Johnson & Johnson.

It's amazing that we've been able to sign up all these brands as clients based on just two things: concept . . . and relationships. They signed on before ever even viewing a Beta version of the Web site. That's because they see who we have alliances with, and who our investors are, and that's enough to get us in the door. Once we're in, our vision and concept have been compelling enough to win over the brand managers. The alliances make a big difference—people always want to work with a winning team.

For the initial nine months of operation, until shortly before the second round of financing, Jeff Malkin ran the company out of his home—and yet still managed to stretch the company's alliances beyond the U.S. borders.

We're concurrently developing joint ventures in the U.K. and Latin America, and have a joint venture we're in the process of signing right now with China. The subsidiary in the U.K. is going to raise up to £12 million as a first round.

Another motivation for partnering is to benefit from a company showing high momentum.

The one other notion relevant to the Internet space is being able to ride the momentum of a partner's coattails as they approach IPO or just after they've IPO'd.

For example, we recently closed a strategic partnership with AllAdvantage.com. They had closed a round of financing in the hundreds of millions and are on the fast track to an IPO and they've got tremendous momentum with 7 million people signed up in just a few months.

With the media and Wall Street so tied into the dot-com world, it's important to partner with the right companies. I want to ride their coattails. I want people to know that FreeSamples.com is partnered with them.

Malkin's strategy appeared to be working. In the first three weeks after launching the Beta test, on word of mouth and media mentions alone, the FreeSamples Web site drew 800,000 unique visitors, earning a ranking as one of the 300 fastest growing sites. During the same three weeks, the company sent out 350,000 samples. All this without any advertising, without yet being listed by any search engine.

Cultural historians fifty or a hundred years from now will write about California as a wellspring of ideas, fads, and phenomena that in time swept the nation, sometimes the world—from health foods and giving up cigarette smoking, to casual dress in the workplace on Fridays and music by the Beach Boys.

While California doesn't have an exclusive claim to making the computer an everyday reality—Digital and IBM, to name just two of the exceptions, were, of course, East Coast companies—still, innovators like Steve and Woz, Hewlett and Packard, and, later, Bill Gates helped lay the West Coast groundwork that sprouted into the phenomenon of high tech and the e-business era. And if you've begun to grasp my underlying theme in this book, e-business isn't just about a new channel for marketing; it's about entirely new ways of running your business.

One of these new ideas that has been more or less launched from within the technology industry is a practice I see as becoming a fundamental, if not an essential, for doing business successfully in the e-business world. Appropriately it was Intel's Andy Grove who coined the clever compound term being adopted as the favorite descriptor of the practice: "coopetition."

Simply put, leading companies are discovering that they can tackle various kinds of problems in cooperation with their traditional competitors while still retaining their active rivalries in other areas. Coopetition equals cooperation plus competition.

Microsoft clearly is a competitor to many organizations that sell various software products; take IBM as one very prominent case in point. Yet at the same time there are many examples where both IBM and Microsoft are involved in a sale. In one particular case that comes to mind, the two companies both bid on selling messaging software to a very large global corporation—IBM proposing their product called Notes, against our electronic messaging product Exchange.

Microsoft won the competition. But the customer then advised that they had a close, long-standing relationship with IBM for worldwide service and support, and it would be a requirement that we work hand in hand with IBM in developing and installing the product. Moreover, the software was to be installed on hardware from various vendors, including IBM.

Microsoft and IBM working *together*? Yes. It was clearly in the best interests of both companies, and, though we still compete intensely for the electronic messaging business as well as in many other areas, we had no problem cooperating to provide the best solution for the customer.

That's coopetition.

It's not uncommon today, as you may well know from your own experience, that IBM is contracted to install Microsoft software on hardware from Hewlett-Packard and other manufacturers. In fact, that's been the case for quite a while in the high-tech industry, because it frequently happens that one supplier doesn't offer all the parts of the solution that the customer needs. A bank may want a specific banking application from one developer, to run under a Microsoft operating system, on hardware from Dell or HP or IBM—or all three. The whole concept of system integration, a huge business in the high-tech field, has often required that multiple suppliers work together to give the customer a complete solution.

But taking it to the next step, where two or more competitors on their own join forces for an effort of common interest?

For some traditional companies, this may sound like a foreign and dangerous idea. Why would a Texaco work with a Mobil, an American Airlines work with United Airlines? A year or three ago you might have figured, Never. Today, you read the headlines about Ford and GM and DaimlerChrysler joining forces to create that procurement exchange for serving the needs of all three, and you recognize another potent sign that the world of business is changing.

Coopetition.

Microsoft's vice president of sales, marketing and service has his own vivid way of describing these new alliances.

Jeff Raikes:

> Now with the horizontal integration of businesses, the new reality is that we are all operating in an environment where one day you're selling against a competitor and the next day you're partnering with them.
>
> So, we desperately want to succeed against Oracle in the database business, yet we desperately want Oracle to put their database on the Windows platform.
>
> **Whoever you meet with at breakfast as a partner may be your competitor at lunch.**

Clearly it's technology that's fueling this—particularly the Internet and the e-commerce phenomenon, and it reinforces the key question: Why should every organization try to enhance their own procurement systems, their own payroll systems, their own finance systems . . . when many of these are essentially generic processes that are not only similar within industries, but similar *across* industries? At the end of the day, does Microsoft, does your own company, really need a payroll system much different than a bank's, or an insurance company's, or an aircraft manufacturing company's?

Other payoffs from coopetition aren't immediately obvious.

For one thing, cooperating with other companies in your industry can yield a powerful benefit in terms of staffing. What's one of the biggest complaints today from organizations trying to take advantage of the technology revolution? Over and over I hear managers complaining they can't find enough technically qualified people. When companies come together as those auto industry firms did to build one procurement system, all the companies involved can reassign technical talent to other, more productive work.

For another, the advantages of a competitive alliance can extend to others who benefit without directly taking part, especially the suppliers and the customers. For suppliers, it means not having to reinvent a different interface, a different process, a different mechanism to sell to the three or four or multiple primary players, but rather relying on a single common standard they all agree to use. That means cost savings for the suppliers, as well.

And the cost savings along the line should in the end play out to the consumer's advantage in a lower price tag on the end product.

In many sales relationships, what customers want goes beyond simply buying your product or service; they want some relationship with your organization, and sometimes they even want to explore ways of going into business with you. To me this seems like a new way of doing business, and I'm fascinated by it.

In Mexico, we've cut a deal with the telephone company to reach out to Spanish-speaking people on the Internet. And Ford Motor Company recently agreed to a joint arrangement with us for a system that makes it easier for customers to link with the Ford dealer network, and helps the dealer build a stronger relationship with the customer.

Today companies come to us regularly to initiate discussions about partnering and strategic-alliance relationships. And sometimes through our focus on individual industries, we reach out to other companies. More and more these relationships go beyond the sale or licensing of software, to become working business alliances. This has become one of the hottest discussion items between our customers and ourselves.

It's worth pausing a moment to recognize that the degree of partnering we're talking about only becomes possible because of the Digital Revolution and the world it creates—one in which people are connected everywhere, connected to everybody, connected all the time. An old expression you no longer hear asserted that there was "nothing new under the sun." But this digital-era level of integration, something that indeed is totally new, allows your company to integrate with competitors, and with suppliers, and with customers, to gain advantages never before possible.

The areas where partnering makes best sense are the areas that don't differentiate the product or service. Even if raw materials and components are procured the same way by the three automobile manufacturers, that doesn't change how they design their vehicles; it doesn't change the competitive advantage that one may exercise over another by having an engineering edge or a more appealing set of product features. So it really lets you focus all of your own resources on those areas that have the most impact on your competitive edge and the most perceived difference at the customer end of the equation.

It's an intriguing process to watch, and requires whole new attitudes and thought processes. But get ready for it, folks—because that's where business is going.

CHAPTER 9

*Most innovative organizations are rapidly
replacing rules with roles . . . and leaving
employees to their own devices, absent rigidity.*

— RICHARD W. OLIVER

It's Not the Technology,
Stupid — It's the Culture

In this new era that we've all entered, Microsoft is a start-up like every other company that's focused on surviving. A start-up in the sense that we've understood the message "Get your act together or you'll disappear." If you want to be a leader in the next round, if you want even to survive *until* the next round, you'll have to earn it.

Walk into a company that has understood the message and you sense it almost as soon as you get through the door. You sense the electricity in the air, a vibrancy, a feeling of urgency, a passion— because companies that understand the future know they can't dawdle about getting there. Personally I can't imagine working in a place that reeks with the aura of nine to five, a place that's a yawn during the day and where the parking lot is empty at night and the lights are only on for the cleaning crew.

I even sense a difference now from city to city. You can tell in the same way the ones that are hurtling toward the new age and the ones that aren't. Fly into San Diego or Austin or Charlotte, North

Carolina, and you sense they're abuzz. Fly into others (it would be really tactless to name any), and you sense they're still waiting to catch on. It's sad that pockets of our country are missing out on this unbelievable, once-in-a-lifetime shift.

Today's high-tech companies are, I believe, models for the corporate culture of the twenty-first century. I want to show you a little of the one I know.

When I was being interviewed to become an executive of Microsoft, I remember one question asked me by Steve Ballmer—who is, of course, now our CEO.

Steve challenged me to look back on my career to that point and tell me about a project I remembered as most exciting to me. I was at the time a partner with Ernst & Young, but the answer I gave actually came from an experience I had as a relatively junior manager at a well-known insurance company.

Back then, in the very early days of technology, I had been working on a project that was an attempt to automate the company's intricate claims process. And we were running into some conflict with the information technology organization, because they saw what we were trying to do as a bit rebellious, stretching the technology, and running a lot of risk. Besides which, they were sure we couldn't get it done when we said we would.

We got it done a lot quicker. This was a company with a four-day workweek; we were putting in six and seven.

I think Steve perhaps heard in that story a dedication for getting the job done no matter what it takes. Apparently the way I answered, the enthusiasm I had in remembering some of the very specific reasons I felt so strongly about a project from many years before, all that was a data point suggesting I might be a good fit here—even though, as a product of a military education (Virginia Military Institute), I was and still am something of an anomaly . . .

and still take occasional teasing for graduating from the same college General Patton attended. (I've taken a little less kidding about that lately, since a major business journal ran a cover story on Steve, comparing him to that same World War II general.)

My other most memorable interview came at a meeting later that day with Bill Gates. I had launched into an explanation of why it would be a good idea to let me stay in San Francisco and work from there. He heard me out for all of about forty-five seconds, said it wouldn't do, and moved on to another topic.

Those interviews—I had several others on that one day, talking both to people I would work for and people I would work with—were my first taste of the Microsoft culture. After going through the process, many people decide they want no more of the place. I thought it would suit my temperament just fine.

Bill Gates, Steve Jobs, and David Packard (cofounder of Hewlett-Packard) each created a company with a kick-ass culture that broke out from hidebound ways of doing business. Three sharply different cultures, each its own version of defining new ways, each stunningly successful despite the occasional setback.

Not long after being hired, my first real introduction to the Microsoft culture, an eye-opener, came at one of the first company meetings I went to. I was still new at the place, still imbued with the values I had brought from the world of corporate consulting.

Microsoft was small then—this was a decade ago—and as part of each annual employee meeting, Bill would stand at the podium, read questions that had been submitted by employees, and answer them in front of the whole staff. It's going along smoothly enough, and then he says into the microphone something like, "This next one is from _____, who works in Building Three, and he writes, 'My favorite drink is . . .' "—and he gives the name of some kind of lemon water I never heard of—" 'and how come it isn't available in the soft-drink coolers?' "

I sit there thinking, Is this guy dumb and blind? He's complaining to the chairman of the company over a stupid brand of soft drink! I'm about to hear somebody get fired in front of the entire workforce!

Not quite. Bill says, "I'm very sorry, I apologize. And by the time you get back from this meeting, it will be in the cooler."

That told me a great deal about the Microsoft culture: Employees are the lifeblood of the organization; we will do just about anything to make them happy—as long as they can handle the pace and the style.

On the other hand, it's no secret that Bill Gates can be very demanding in his expectations of the people around him. His mix of business talent and technical knowledge is matched by a memory that's a trap for everything he ever heard. Which is why I say you have not been through a business review until you've come through one with him. His command of the information is amazing.

Microsoft's executive vice president and chief operating officer notes how another part of the Bill Gates character has formed the character of the company.

Bob Herbold:

Our chairman is one tight dude, which has shaped a company that's into the practical, not into the lush. That's become a fabric of our company and we all take great pride in being efficient. We want to have great facilities for our people, but great means a comfortable, good workplace, a good place for them to be creative.

Another driving principal that has shaped the Microsoft culture, and continues to shape it, is the emphasis on simplifying our business systems and processes.

Bob Herbold was involved in one effort that turned out to be an early impetus pushing the company toward the idea of simplifying.

Bob Herbold:

> *We had this horrific mess in Finance because we had started doing business in all these countries, and all of a sudden we realized they were all sending us financial reports, often using different data definitions and spreadsheets.*
>
> *The Germans were defining their market and costs one way and the French another way, each country doing its own thing, and all sending their data to us in different formats.*
>
> *These differences were most evident at the end of the quarter when we had to close the books. Our Finance people were going nuts just trying to close the quarter. That's when you blow the whistle and say, Time for a fresh sheet of paper.*

As we explore extensively elsewhere in these pages, any company can achieve substantial improvements by simplifying not just paperwork but—as Bob Herbold points out—processes as well, especially those involving IT.

> *A lot of companies get the job done by basically building systems on top of systems, with more and more paper forms and complicated reports. You reach a point when you need to throw the whole mess away and say, "Okay, we'll just start with a fresh sheet of paper." You design a simple, up-to-date approach with Web interface, not forms.*
>
> *Then you take the next step and eliminate the people who used to answer the phone about handling those forms. In fact, you have to eliminate that old process and only have the new one; otherwise you've driven up your costs significantly.*
>
> *If you're going to minimize information systems to significantly cut costs, you then have to eliminate systems developers, because—*
>
> **Systems developers are like rabbits. If you have systems developers, you get more systems. That's what they do for a living!**

> *Out in the geographies, your IT people should be there to support the global systems that are being used within those countries; they should not have sufficient manpower to develop new systems.*

This effort goes beyond simplifying just for the sake of simplifying, says our group VP for sales.

Jeff Raikes:

We have a strong sense of wanting to tie the use of the technology to particular business goals.

For example, all the way back in about 1993, I was frustrated by the fact that our people around the world couldn't really monitor the status of their sales or their revenue versus a set of key goals.

It's challenging in part because we are primarily an indirect sales organization, meaning we sell to distributors who then sell to resellers who then sell to the customers. And so how do you know how effective your sales organization is when you have multiple layers that you're going through, when ultimately what you want is to make sure that you're being successful with the customers?

I put in place a data warehouse system that allows people to know how they're doing. And that developed into an internal program we call MS Sales.

Today, MS Sales stands as a prime example of technology at the service of a business goal.

You have caught on by now that e-mail is used at Microsoft rather differently than in most other organizations.

Along with other company executives, I have for years been taking part in those Microsoft CEO Summits, to which the company invites chief executives from around the world. Some of what our guests hear from us and from Bill Gates about the way we do things at Microsoft astounds them.

Jeff Raikes:

> *Bill and others have told the stories at these sessions about how our company runs, and the free form, free flow of information. It's interesting to see how the CEOs react. It's like, "You mean anybody in my company could e-mail me? That's not acceptable." Just total shock.*
>
> *That's the initial reaction. But there have been a number of people—I think perhaps John Bryson of Edison International was one—who have come to the CEO Summit, gone back, had their e-mail account set up, and sent word out that they were reading their e-mail from employees.*
>
> *To me that's an example of the change in work process and work culture that can be nurtured by technology, that takes advantage of technology.*

Along the same lines, I've had people say things like, "Junk mail going to Mr. Gates and Mr. Balmer! Boy, that would never work at my company. How do you manage?" I guess that kind of remark presumes a lot of our folks are really brain-dead and would actually send junk mail to the chairman and the CEO. We've made this crazy assumption that most of ours are not brain-dead—and what do you know, it actually works out to be a great system, good for the employees and occasionally bringing us some great idea or leading to some important direction for the company.

We're glad to have people shoot off their e-mails to any manager or executive in the company, without anybody's permission. Somewhere in there will be the occasional kernel of a brilliant idea that will help the company. We want to encourage that, not impede it.

In view of this style of communicating, I sometimes describe the functioning of this company as an egalitarian debating society that can transform in an instant into an absolute dictatorship. Our chief operating officer has his own views on how open debate should work.

Bob Herbold:

> *You get a lot of bright ideas. But what's important in a process like that is to know who it is that's in position to say, "Thanks for the input, we're done." If you don't have clarity around that, you're in trouble.*
>
> *And I can guarantee you one of the reasons why we've driven a lot of efficiencies in our core processes is that we know exactly who it is who's been given the power to say that, in each area of the company. Those people have my complete backing. And so the person in HR or the person in Finance who drives those processes, they know when it's time to say, "Enough, I've considered all your input, we'll now do what I've decided to do."*

People hearing this are inclined to say something like, "Microsoft is famous for its innovation, but that sounds like it has a march-in-step rigidity to it." The response to that is easy.

Bob Herbold:

> *Our people are really good at knowing when it's time to be creative and when it's time to take orders. This is something that's very interesting: we really do know that when the person with authority on a particular issue says, "We're going to do this," everybody salutes.*
>
> *It's a very unusual mix of knowing when it is that we have to be disciplined and march to one drummer, and when it is that we need to turn on the creative juices and be innovative.*

Make-or-break decisions today face most companies in seemingly unending succession. To name just one that Microsoft has contended with, I've heard vivid stories about the tremendous uncertainty over switching from the kludgy but familar DOS commands to a graphical user interface of icons and menus: Would customers embrace the change, or rebel and flee? Would developers, faced with extensive rewriting of their programs, support us, or let us hang out in the breeze with few applications to run on the new operating system? In the early years, Windows was anything but a home run, making a lot of Microsoft people very, very nervous.

In the end Bill's decision proved sound.

And today we face another of those monumental, bet-the-farm efforts. Announced in the summer of 2000 under the name •NET (spoken as "dot-Net"), it assumes that many, if not most, computer users in coming years won't spend their time working as today with application programs like Word and Excel on their own machines, but will do the same work online in some kind of Internet super-browser that provides access to all the same application capabilities.

Providing users with this ability will require that our company rewrite almost all of its software so that it suits the Internet environment while still maintaining compatibility with traditional desktop use. Once again we're taking a huge risk that this is something customers will want. If not . . .

A company's culture is the summation of certain characteristics of the management, plus characteristics of the employees. The culture of Microsoft has in part been shaped by the way our people view technology.

Jeff Raikes:

> Certainly a very important part of this is an openness to the use of technology. But in our case, it's even more accurately described as a passion *for how technology can be used and applied. Our company is made up of a lot of people who think software is cool, that it can do wonderful things for people. And I think that makes us very open-minded.*

The idea of *passion* plays in other senses, as well. I say to new employees after they've been here a couple of months, "If you have not picked up some passion about this place, some enthusiasm, even recognizing how over the top we are in a zillion ways, then you've missed it, you probably aren't going to make it here." Microsoft is a place that gives a lot to people—and more than just financially— but it's also a place that asks a lot. For anybody who has an I'm-just- here-for-the-paycheck attitude, Microsoft isn't likely to be a comfortable fit.

How do you establish the sort of corporate culture where people are willing to work ridiculous hours, put out a Herculean effort not just on one project but continually, practically nonstop for months on end, striving to create software that meets the Bill Gates goal of moving toward a world where everyone has access to the network, any time, anywhere? That only happens if you can manage to create a sense of loyalty.

And I think that kind of loyalty is only nurtured in an environ- ment where the employees clearly see the company truly cares about their welfare.

The perks are awesome. In 1985, when Microsoft was preparing to go public (this was before I joined the company), Bill and his executive team were faced with creating a stock option plan for employees. Steve Ballmer once told me how the decisions were made. He said, "We had no experience and we were wondering how to do it. We brought in the usual suspects to consult with us, and they came back with plans like those at every other company."

Some consultants, he said, recommended what you would expect—big stock packages for the CEO and other founders, and very handsome packages for the executives. Steve told me, "At the end of the day, we decided on a system that would make every employee eligible for stock options, calculated with the hope that after four and a half years of vesting, Microsoft employees, even people at lower levels, would have at least enough money to put a down payment on a house."

Here was a company founded by people who said, Hey, we're all in this together.

The admin who has been with me for some years now, Teri

Jensen, was a waitress in a Black Angus restaurant when she was hired by Microsoft. For a year she worked both jobs—making more in tips in the evenings than working twice as many hours as a Microsoft inventory clerk. But thanks to this company's employee stock program, after sixteen years here she's financially independent . . . yet having so much fun that she still comes to work for me every day. (She has a quick laugh, much quicker than most secretaries I've ever met, and maybe all that stock has something to do with this happy characteristic!)

I've heard of very few companies other than small start-ups that ever shared the wealth on such a scale before Microsoft.

Not with the same level of impact, but the perks go beyond stock options. Most employees have their own office—in very nice surroundings. Okay, so they're not plush: My office is essentially the same as my admin's and everyone else's—same quality of furniture, same plain walls, same drab carpeting. The only difference between my office and any other employee's is that mine has enough extra space for a coffee table with chairs around it.

The company cafeterias serve three meals a day, five days a week. And we periodically bring in local chefs to prepare their specialties. Recently a renowned chef, Gene Porter of Dixie Barbeque, a restaurant widely known throughout the county, was on campus serving up ribs with his special, very hot sauce known as "the Man."

And—one of the things we get kidded about by visitors, especially by our customers—in every building on campus (and there are now over fifty of them), we have a series of what amount to mini convenience stores. There isn't a nonalcoholic drink or variety of water you can name that you won't find, chilled and available for the taking—all free, along with all sorts of candy bars, snacks, coffee, tea, you name it. The refreshment areas are kept fully stocked twenty-four hours a day, seven days a week.

Yes, I'll admit this is not just being "nice" but rather honoring the wisdom that the higher the quality of the work environment, the more effort employees will put in to get the job done. It's part of the inducement for putting in extra hours to ensure we stay a few steps ahead of the competition. (Still, people here put in so much effort that one journalist referred to Microsoft in print as "the velvet sweat shop.")

Every company says their employees are the most important asset, blah, blah, blah. In a software company—not just Microsoft, but any software company, and most service organizations, as well—your employees are the only asset you have. A software company sells ones and zeros. That's essentially our entire product line—ones and zeros. We have some land and a whole bunch of buildings and several thousand desktop computers (though they're written off to a zero value after one year). Those things don't add up to a market cap exceeding a quarter of a trillion dollars—that comes from the intellectual property.

So the only asset we have is the intellectual capacity, the brains, of our workers. Other companies can claim the employees are their chief asset, but we don't have much of anything else.

Yet in a way this fact gives us one big advantage over traditional businesses: It makes us face up to a commitment to employees that's more than just a figure of speech.

There's no reason this thinking has to be limited to software and service organizations. Both Dell and Cisco, to name just two examples, have emulated Microsoft with their stock sharing programs and in other ways.

This Microsoft culture ain't perfect, and the downside is it can, as I've said, be more than a little "in your face." But the flip side is that the company really does try to build a support structure, a benefits environment, and a sharing of the wealth at a level that I believe has never been done before.

Still the question remains: What contributes to giving Microsoft so strong a culture, what differentiates the company? Every senior manager has his or her own answer. Here's one.

Jeff Raikes:

Part of it is the fact that we're basically revolutionaries. I have no experience in corporate America—I grew up on a farm and then I went to Apple computer, and then came here. So my life experiences don't help me understand what those traditional corporate cultures are like.

But I think in some sense that's a part of the answer. You have a bunch of guys who grew up wanting to change the world, and here we are still trying to change the world.

I'm trying to think of a better adjective than saying "coolness." But, you know, we hire a lot of people out of college, meaning our average age here is probably thirty-two, thirty-three years old. So it's very important that we not just develop technology but we try things ourselves, so people feel, "Wow, it's cool to work at Microsoft." Microsoft's willing to be on the leading edge and do things in new ways.

Certainly by using new technology ourselves, we have the hands-on experience every day with using these technologies to improve our own productivity, to improve our business success. There's a phrase popular in high tech that Steve [Ballmer] sometimes uses: "Eating your own dog food." I prefer the phrase, "Eating your own cooking." But the bottom line is, by using advanced technologies ourselves, we are that much better positioned to be able to help our customers understand the benefits.

As an example, all the Microsoft buildings are currently being equipped to allow wireless connecting, so we're able to carry a laptop anywhere on campus and connect to our desktop computers or download our e-mail, without having to plug in to a telephone outlet. When our customers begin using wireless, we'll already be in touch with the users' perspective.

People every now and then suggest that Microsoft has some inherent cultural advantage that wouldn't work in other companies— "That's fine with Microsoft, but it really won't work here."

In fact, Microsoft people agree it would not necessarily work elsewhere.

Jeff Raikes:

> *Different business missions do require different cultures. Because we are basically an intellectual property firm, the kind of culture we encourage here is very much designed for the free flow of thought, whereas if you're in a thin-margin service organization business the culture has to be driven around tight operations. Yet in both cases, the flow of information is such that it can have a significant contribution to the achievement of the business mission.*
>
> *So there will be differences in culture and access, but nothing in terms of how technology is applied to the work processes that couldn't be replicated. You just have to have the will. A lot of companies don't have the will. They'll achieve it ultimately or they'll be out of business.*

In the end, what is it that allows a company to be rigid and demanding in some aspects, yet open, nurturing, and creative in others?

Bob Herbold:

> *What happens in life, in the way human beings are wired, is that even if two people are assigned to the exact same task, they will each take a lot of pride in the creativity of how they exercise the responsibility. So they won't do the task the same way.*
>
> *And what we try to do here at Microsoft is sort out those items that are actually just procedural or process oriented, as opposed to those that really need the innovation. The procedural things, everybody should be doing the same way.*
>
> *Clearly the products or services that are being offered to customers need to benefit from controlled creativity and innovation, to be better than our competition.*

.   .   .

On the issue of culture, sometimes outsiders see a company more clearly than its own people do. An author came to visit Microsoft and we gave him free reign of the campus. He interviewed some of the exec staff, and he stopped a lot of people around the campus to chat.

When he was wrapped up, he dropped by to share a little of his experience. What had surprised him most, he said, came when he asked people questions like, "What are the threats you face today, what concerns you most?"

The answers he got, time after time, were along the lines of, "I get up in the morning worried that somebody's about to kill us. I worry all day that we've built this great thing but we might be dead meat tomorrow."

He said, "It was bizarre—here I am at the headquarters of the most successful company on Earth, most of the people are probably worth a great deal of money, yet every one of you is worried sick it's all going to be snatched away tomorrow by competitors who come up with products that are neater, cooler, more appealing."

Where does that "they're catching up, we have to move forward *fast*" attitude come from? You guessed it, of course—the attitude originally came from Bill himself. He's told us repeatedly, "Don't take anything for granted. Unless we work every day convinced someone's treading on our heels, someone will be there treading on our heels."

That paranoia the reporter detected all over the campus isn't delusional. Microsoft people truly do believe that with one false step we could lose it all. Their job isn't just to develop a new product or a new marketing program, it's to make damned sure the company doesn't get killed by the competition.

I don't think this company is going to start sliding downhill tomorrow or the next day or the day after that, but keeping everyone so focused has, I think, created an environment where we are all in a start-up mentality. Bill Gates has shaped a culture that doesn't grow complacent. It's a strength and not a weakness to have people understand this message: Take nothing for granted, get up every day paranoid about the threats to the survival of the company, and figure out what you have to do to prevent "the end of Microsoft" from happening.

So—How do you volunteer to become a guerrilla warrior in the Digital Revolution? For my answer, just look at the title of this chapter. You join the revolution not by buying technology but by adapting the culture of your organization.

CHAPTER 10

The world hates change, yet it is the only thing that has brought progress.

—CHARLES KETTERING

Today, to love change, tumult, even chaos is a prerequisite for survival, let alone success.

—TOM PETERS

Reshaping a Tradition-Bound Corporate Culture

We laid the groundwork in the last chapter for arguing that the entire culture of the organization must change. The same in many cases applies to the management structure, as well. In practice, in the real, day-to-day world where business decisions are made, how does that translate into "What do I do now?"

I still see companies writing three- and even five-year business plans. Incredible!—the marketplace will look so very different five years out that you might as well be asking for guidance from a gypsy fortune-teller.

Even if you believe the technology advances in the next three to five years aren't going to continue at the same frenetic pace we've been witnessing, the handwriting is on the wall: Rapid change is here to stay.

How are organizations adapting to this new world of constant change? What are some leading organizations and top executives doing to enhance change in their own organizations?

Finding the answer begins with understanding the problem clearly.

Archie Kane of Lloyds TSB laughs at what he sees going on today. "A lot of companies have been saying, 'Okay, we need to change to be doing e-business,' but that doesn't necessarily mean they've adopted the attitude of constant change. There are lots of examples of people throwing up a Web page," he says, "but too often it's nothing more than putting their existing marketing catalogues online, or moving their sales process online.

"They're not seeing e-commerce as dramatically changing the business—it's being seen as just another tool."

Foot-dragging about adopting technology innovations is, of course, nothing new. As a vice president at Baxter International in the late 1970s after he left the U.S. Air Force, three-star general Warren D. (Don) Johnson found resistance to the very idea of an executive using a computer. "No corporate officers had any computer equipment for their own use. That amazed me." He had the company purchase a desktop machine and a laptop for him. But "one of the vice presidents came in one day and asked why I was 'wasting my time on the computer.' "

As his final position on active military duty, General Johnson had been director of the Defense Nuclear Agency; in that role, "I had been on the ARPA Net [an early ancestor of today's Internet]. It impressed me as a coming thing, but I thought it was years away from having any wider value—it was so difficult to get much information out of it—for example, if I wanted to know what progress a contractor was making."

At Baxter, his experience with the ARPA Net led the general to order a PC for each executive in his division and to set up a communication system linking them. "A few people," he says, "resisted this with vigor—generally the older employees, who seemed to be afraid they would show their ignorance."

When General Johnson proposed holding no more staff meetings because computer-to-computer communications had made them unnecessary, the people uncomfortable with change complained, "We don't want to do away with the staff meetings, we want to see you face-to-face." He canceled the meetings, anyway. The main outcome, he reports, was that "we saved an enormous amount of time."

Typically, people at levels below senior management were using technology much more than the leaders. But once the COO started using a computer, other executives gradually recognized he had data they didn't, which proved a powerful inducement. Even more powerful: They began to realize their own people had better information, were generally better clued in about what was going on elsewhere in the company.

By the time Don Johnson left, almost every officer was using a computer. Their use, though, was limited to "hardly anything beyond spreadsheet info."

That same kind of progression is being repeated today, this time in the adoption of e-business. But with one humongous difference: The transformation will not happen at so leisurely a pace.

During the time I was writing this book I made a trip to Europe, where I had been requested to speak to the CIOs and executives of twenty-five major corporations. In essence what they wanted to hear was, Why do you think we have to understand e-business and the Digital Revolution, and what happens to a company that doesn't get it?

From my conversations before the speech and after it, and the questions during the Q&A, I calculated there were four companies that already had the message before I arrived. At the end of the day, when the executives of those twenty-five companies left, there were *still* only four companies that understood. The twenty-one companies that arrived in the dark were still in the dark when they left.

Needless to say, the problem is not confined to European companies; I cite the experience as just one example.

Part of the difficulty is that managers and executives don't want to believe they have to change so radically. It's a cliché that change is scary; radical change is scary to the max. I understand that; all of us, even the most adaptable, suffer from the same malady in some areas of our lives—me included.

People who are resisting the e-business phenomenon believe, I think, that even if e-business becomes necessary, their company will have time to react: "We might have it wrong, but it doesn't matter, we can catch up if we have to." So the problem is a combination of "I don't want to" and "I don't have to do it now."

Younger people, of course, generally understand the need earlier than their seniors (they even know how to program a VCR!). But it's not enough for the middle managers of an organization to understand, it's not even enough for the CEO and executive staff to understand. Until the members of the board grasp the scope of the changes coming, and the changes needed within the business, there's little hope.

The customer base is evolving—not the kind of evolution we're familiar with when social forces and shifting mores bring gradual transitions, but grand, dramatic, galactic changes, largely induced by the Internet.

This point was brought home on a fascinating CBS television special in which the producers took a couple of young people, put them in an apartment in Houston with a telephone line and a PC, turned on the cameras, and followed them over the course of a week to see if they could furnish the place, get linens, soap, dishes, and toilet paper sent in, get their food delivered, and generally live out the week without stepping across the threshold. And, of course, they did.

Not that I think a lot of people are going to become hermits just because technology makes it possible, but it's already clear how drastically buying habits are going to change. Tomorrow's consumers will have a much different view of the need to go out to a familiar brick-and-mortar store or shopping mall, to the corner bank, even to the supermarket. They'll have a much different idea about whether they need to be face-to-face with a salesperson before buying a car. And about how they will do volunteer work with the organizations they belong to. And about how they interact with their political representatives. And even about how they form their opinions and cast their votes in local, state, and national elections.

Who is that man behind the curtain? Tomorrow's consumers won't even ask: They'll take the miracles of technology as much for granted as we take the telephone, the automobile and the in-flight traffic reports on television.

Companies that have been early adopters in moving to a Digital Era/e-business environment have had to find their own ways of bringing about change in the workforce. Others now have the benefit of learning from their trials and successes.

The familiar problem of a workforce fearing change became a challenge for management at the stock brokerage firm of Merrill Lynch not long ago, a situation made worse when change was thrust on the workers unexpectedly. The first vice president and chief technology officer of the Merrill Lynch Private Client Architecture group described what happened.

Tony Pizi:

> *There was significant fear among the more successful financial consultants because they had established patterns with their clients, they were doing*

well and they were comfortable with their situation. And anything that threatened to change this relationship would naturally raise some concern.

The big question, as always, in this discussion: how was the change message conveyed?

There were a lot of things. I think senior management took the communication very seriously. At every Recognition Club, where you get the most successful financial consultants, there was steady and increasing emphasis on technology, on the effects of technology, how to leverage technology, and so forth. Executives began spending a lot of time with this; technology began to take center stage. It was a process over a two- or three-year period. And then once it happened, internally the reaction wasn't, Oh, this is going to crush us, but more of, Okay, let's get on with it.

Also, as we put out Merrill Lynch Online, we also put out better tools, and provided a platform for collaboration. The consultants found that with their clients who started to use Merrill Lynch Online, they had more meaningful dialogues, they had a better basis for engaging the client. Before, they might have called up and said, "Look, we just came out with some new research on Intel, I'd like to send you a copy and then go over it with you."

Instead of that dialogue, now there might be an alert e-mail to the client, who would go in and look at the research online. So the first real conversation the consultant had was after both of them had already had the chance to assimilate the information. The level of conversation was more efficient, a higher bandwidth, taking the mundane and trivial from their plate and moving them to a place where they were dealing with more substantive issues.

That was something our consultants found surprising. And the overall client satisfaction shot up significantly for the clients who used the online services.

The best thing about this has been that the success is emulated—the financial consultants who were developing new patterns, who were leveraging the technology, those individuals were quickly emulated by others in the office and others in the branch system.

I think all companies are faced with the kinds of issues Merrill has been faced with—especially successful companies. The bar has just been raised on us all.

Pizi also added a personal note—not particularly germane to the discussion, but I couldn't resist including this.

It's funny, my own account is very different than the college accounts for my kids. I know that I have an obligation for them in eight or ten years and so theirs are much more diversified. With my own account I can be more aggressive. It's different bowls for different needs. I'm much more inclined to take the advice and guidance of my financial consultant for my kids' account than for mine, which I consider more like fun. And I let the kids know every time they outperform me. But when it's the other way around, I just smile to myself.

The name Coles Myer is as familiar to an Australian as McDonald's or Coca-Cola are to Americans. One of the world's leading retailers, the company owns department stores, discount stores, specialty shops, food stores, liquor stores, and fast food outlets. In other words, Coles Myer is a cross section of the entire retailing industry. Incredibly, it takes in twenty cents of every dollar that's spent in Australia at retail. The company has annual revenues of A$23 billion—roughly equivalent to U.S.$13 billion, making it about the size of Goodyear Tire or Atlantic Richfield, companies well up the list of the Fortune 500.

Leading Coles Myer as CEO is Dennis Eck, an American from Wolf Point, Montana. The town is "fifty miles south of Canada and one hundred miles west of North Dakota," he likes to say. "The traders used to bring their hides down to a point in Missouri where the riverboats came up the river to collect them every year, which is the way the town got its name."

Nobody has a corner on the market for innovative thinking. It just comes more naturally to some people than to others, the same as playing the piano, stroking on the links in the 90s, or writing a publishable novel. And like those other abilities, innovative thinking, I'm convinced, can with enough determination be mastered.

It helps to pick up tips from experts. In my view, Coles Myer CEO Dennis Eck qualifies as an innovation expert. What's more, how can you not be just a little in awe of a man who went from a political science and history background to become a marketing executive at Vons, and finally to head one of Australia's most notable firms? As you might expect, he's a man whose background influences the way he sees the challenges of making business decisions. That background has led him to some contrarian views.

Dennis Eck:

> *History and political science are good training for business. History teaches you that there's a value in learning from what's gone on in the past. But that's not worth much unless it helps you predict and make better decisions in the future.*

(Carved in stone over the entrance to the National Archives Building in Washington, D.C., is the saying, "What is past is prologue." It's another way of expressing Dennis Eck's judgment about the value of history.)

> *Political science teaches us that there are huge numbers of different ways of organizing human behavior. The key is to figure out how to involve the people in the process of setting rules, standards, cultures—that's the way you get people to function together as a community.*
>
> *So history and political science are actually two very good disciplines for the technological era, where things are moving so quickly that people sometimes don't bother to check on the output of their previous decisions.*

In Dennis Eck's view, the rest of us have things backward in believing that companies need to change their culture in response to advances in technology.

I don't think technology ever requires a culture change. I think the culture change requires technology.

This concept of a culture change—what is it, really? There's an old Russian proverb that says that the wolf is near but the czar is far. We employ 150,000 people and have nearly 2,000 outlets. I would have to be a very powerful person in order to push my ideas through that mass.

The way we've been using technology at Coles Myer—for example, our focus on selling to customers as a market of one—requires a whole different way of considering how we sell goods. Technology comes in because it allows us to understand the market at that level. It also allows us to engage our employees to that level. And third, technology then is efficient in the supply chain because it allows us to ship only the items needed by that particular store.

At no point in our past have we had today's ability to bring all of that to bear on something as simple as selling somebody a product. And we'd be silly not to use it, right?

Though Dennis Eck insists that culture change drives technology, he has still found brilliant ways to change the typical culture of retailing by taking advantage of technology.

I have a view that ideas actually cascade up now rather than cascade down. And that that's the real power of information technology and the real power of what's going on in the world today.

We take a nineteen-year-old kid and our first step is to put him in charge of an aisle or two in a store—say, the pet food aisles. Our purpose is to give the youngster a chance to understand how those products sell in his or her neighborhood, understand the pricing that's relevant in the neighborhood, and understand how the allocation of that section could be made better for the customer so the items are in stock most of the time.

The youngster then feeds up into the computer the assortment he wants to stock, and it comes through to the buyers, and they buy the items and have them distributed to his store.

So we've enabled the buying decisions to be made where the knowledge exists. We then build comprehensive support structures to allow the sum total of those decisions to be the strategy of that business.

We've engaged this nineteen-year-old at a young age, allowed him to use the computer, and allowed him to have a sense that the objectives he's set for himself can be met.

The buyers now can focus on finding the new trends, the new items, and the things that should be added into the assortment.

Most companies would take that pet food data, move it up into their major computer, and do an analysis of it. And the result—the assortment and the pricing that makes sense for most of the chain—they would distribute back down to the stores and say, "This is what your pet food aisle should look like."

Our way, the youngsters in each of the stores say, "This is what my pet food aisle looks like." And we distribute that knowledge back up. And then the computer allows us to control that process so we maintain control of the assortment, the pricing, the shrink, and all of the things that we need to run a good business.

We also feed into that knowledge base the things they couldn't know at the store level: What are consumers thinking about their pets? What are the new trends in pet food? And we give that to the kid who's running the pet food section so he or she can make better decisions.

But when we're executing, we go back to being a hierarchy again. The kid still has to meet our payroll objective, he still has to meet our margin target, and he still has to meet those control mechanisms that businesses need to sustain profitability—all while he makes his aisle fit into the community.

The underlying element, and I think it's the hardest part for everyone, is that we actually have to trust the people doing the work—which is not something that most organizational structures are built around.

Whether the chicken came first or the egg, Dennis Eck isn't sure.

I don't know whether technology causes this or people cause it and technology just participates. But the notion of putting a lot more authority at the lower levels is so contrary to the way most organizational people think of using employees that it sounds counterintuitive. But it works, so how could it be wrong!

Where most people are using the computer to distribute decisions, what in effect we've done is use the computer to control distributed decisions.

Extending, or perhaps modifying, his description of information traveling up and down the chain, Dennis went on to suggest that the key distinction is this—

Most knowledge is distributed from the center outward. We're actually starting where knowledge exists, distributing it backwards and enhancing it.

It's interesting isn't it—as if we were asking, "What other purpose can a computer have?" But if you think about it, we're beginning to attack some of the fundamental precepts of hierarchical organizations.

People in the middle have to get used to a simple idea: It's highly likely that somebody below them actually has more knowledge to apply to the problem than they have.

Information places older employees under pressure because analytical power now exists at these lower levels. In most organizations, once something is wrong about the data, it's hard to keep everything from being wrong. And that discordance is what's sowing the seeds of lack of belief in the corporation as an institution today.

Major General Anthony Raper runs the British military's Defence Communication Services Agency, responsible for providing information and communication services worldwide. To do that job, the agency employs some thirty-four hundred military and civilian personnel.

Sometimes you find people who promote change in unexpected places. But I've known Tony Raper long enough not to be surprised by his vision, his persuasiveness, or his effectiveness.

General Raper:

> *We would see ourselves very much as the enablers of change in terms of moving the Ministry of Defence towards an e-business approach whereby it fully exploits the benefits of modern information technology.*
>
> *Some people get upset if I'm the one who says, "You have to change." So my approach to that is to talk about, "How do we enable the change?" and "How can we transform Defence through the use of information?"*
>
> *I'm quite clear that I'm not the chief knowledge officer for the Ministry of Defence. I'm equally quite clear that I will deliver a great deal of the technology that will enable people to manage knowledge better. It naturally follows that I need people in my organization who really understand the business of defense—both in terms of being a government department, and also in terms of military operations. This is critical if we are to enable Defence to exploit the information revolution.*
>
> *I believe the military will soon go through some quite significant changes. Not simply the changes in terms of the combat power that is available and how it might be employed, but in people's ability to access information in a nonhierarchical way. This will lead to changes in processes and changes in structures.*

But General Raper shares the view that technology remains a stumbling block for many.

> *Many government organizations still have decision makers who are predominantly what I would describe as "technophobic." They tend to see information technology in terms of big bang projects that have failed, rather than as projects which, correctly managed, have brought huge benefits.*
>
> *In contrast, I remember the chairman of one of our major banks describing how they made the decision to take an e-business route. He said that at board level, they made the decision in five minutes, because it was quite simply win or die. They understood the business imperative that the technology could enable.*
>
> *It is to an extent a continual battle to get people to understand the*

operational and business benefits of the technology and to prevent them
getting lost in the technology itself. The only reason we exploit the technol-
ogy is for those benefits.

If so many people resist technology changes, how do you move them? Lawrence Baxter, who is executive vice president and head of the e-business Division of Wachovia Bank, a regional financial institution in the southeastern United States, uses "change agents."

Lawrence Baxter:

Change agents are people who are willing to work at change on a constant
basis and who are also willing to empathize and understand the psychology
of people resistant to change. They're people who live and thrive on uncer-
tainty. I think people like this are necessary to be the catalyst, to help resist-
ant people get on to the next model.

But just having these change agents isn't enough.

Many companies I think have failed or are failing because they don't moti-
vate those change agents; instead, they punish them either by not promot-
ing them or accepting the characterization of them as being people who are
out in left field, who are unreliable and harebrained.

We have a supportive CEO and senior executive management who have
been able to say, "Yes, we know some of the things that Baxter and others
are saying sounds kooky, but we also know they are not crazy and we want
you to listen to them."

And then they steadily reward these people who are the agents for
change. I've been rewarded by the company visibly and people have seen
that, and it's made my job easier. It's enabled me to persuade people to per-
ceive the strategic need to engage in big change and say, "You won't lose
your job, your career's not going to get into a dead end if you are willing to
push the envelope on these things. On the contrary, you will be rewarded."

How does this actually work in practice? Larry Baxter offered an example.

> In a presentation one time, I said, "We're in an era of tumultuous change and it's creating enormous anxiety, it's making it very difficult for us to plan, but the bad news is that this is going to be the permanent situation going forward." I also talked about the Internet so radically threatening some of our businesses that it could quite possibly destroy some of them.
>
> I think these statements would have just been written off. But our CEO made it very clear that he accepted them—which stopped people who would otherwise have gone around saying, "That Baxter, he's just a crazed ex-academic."
>
> When you get CEO support like that, it's very empowering.

Some leaders take a very straightforward, "here it is" approach to encouraging a technology culture change. As president of Longwood College, a small (thirty-three hundred students) state school tucked in close to the Blue Ridge Mountains, Dr. Patricia P. Cormier has used that kind of head-on approach, but at the same time found ways to smooth the path.

Dr. Cormier:

> Five years ago this institution made the decision to put a computer on the desk of every faculty member. The college purchased the computers and then hired a person from the faculty, an "early adopter," and put that person in charge of something called the Instructional Teaching and Learning Laboratory. He became the catalyst, and went out and identified other early adopters among the faculty to come in and form a team of individuals. Together they slowly but methodically began to integrate technology into the campus.

Dr. Cormier learned one dominant lesson from this process:

Continuous access to a computer is number one in the change process. If it's part-time access, if it's limited access, change doesn't happen.

That's because you have to give people the ability to try, to make mistakes, to fail on their own, to learn not to be afraid of this technology. If you look at three-year-olds, they have absolutely no fear when they walk up to a computer. What's the worse thing that they could do to it? Oh, probably shut it down. But adults don't operate that way. They're concerned that if they touch this button or that one, somehow all their work is going to disappear.

And secondly, we didn't go out and hire an outside technology guru. We gave ongoing training through our own faculty—people the other faculty members already knew and respected.

Baxter International, mentioned earlier in this chapter, was also the site of some novel but powerful ideas that reshaped views on how people in a work group communicate. This was based on innovations of the remarkable Fernando Flores, a teacher, consultant, and author (his most recent book is *Disclosing New Worlds*). Flores holds a Ph.D. in communications and, of all things, had at one time been the minister of finance in Chile, under Salvador Allende.

His work at Baxter started with a three-day course for the company executives, focusing on why so many good ideas died on the vine. He explained one key point by asking people to compare two conversations.

Fernando Flores:

You and I meet on an airplane, we exchange information in the usual way, and discover a business opportunity we might be able to pursue to the benefit of both our companies. I say "Let's get together and talk some more."

We walk off the plane together, and never speak again.

Suppose instead I said, "I'm going to be in your city on business the sixteenth of next month. Can you meet me for dinner at Barney's at seven?" If he's available and agrees, you've taken an important step toward moving ahead on the project.

Basic human communication requires requests and promises. Most of all, it requires *specifics* about what I will do, and what you will do. (It's noteworthy that this notion of insisting on specifics in communicating is also a basic tenet in the work of Silicon Valley consultant and wife of my co-author, Dr. Arynne Simon, who advises, "Without numbers, there is no communication.")

Those specifics form the cornerstone of promises; in a positive, effective corporate culture, promises made are promises to be respected. How employees view each other is based on sincerity, competence, and consistent reliability. And an organization that adheres to those values will come to be recognized for them by customers, suppliers, and investors.

Flores eventually installed at Baxter a software program of his own design that brings up reminders every day of the promises you have made and not yet fulfilled, and promises that have been made to you.

In any organization, there will be some people much slower than others to thaw in the face of change. Those who stay frozen can impede the process for many. How have some of the organizations we've been following surmounted this particular hurdle?

General Raper:

> There is a challenge here for anyone trying to bring about change where those at the top are not as at ease with change as they might be. The answer, I think, is to find a high-level champion who is prepared to push change through. The champion must be able to explain the business benefits of the change and ideally the entire role of the technology. They must not allow themselves to become lost in the technology.
>
> Not surprisingly, you run up against skeptics. For that reason it's invariably important to start by making small changes in a small element of the organization. If people can see it, dare I say touch it and feel it in terms of change, then they sense that much more comfort themselves about being

involved in the whole process. If you are successful, they will become the advocates of change.

What do you do if you can't go above and ordain change from the highest level?

You try to engineer change from the middle. You clearly need people who can recognize the benefits and effects of that change. Anything that you might do to demonstrate the benefits will clearly help you sell your cause.

So one thing that I look to do in terms of U.K. Defence is to make my organization a model of e-business best practice.

It's accepted wisdom that the young have always adapted to change more readily than their elders. (Which reminds me of Churchill's line, which goes something like, "Any man of twenty who isn't a liberal has no heart, and any man of forty who isn't a conservative has no mind.")

Lawrence Baxter, of Wachovia Bank:

Humans are creatures of habit and territory and so the easiest people to bring into this are the youngest and the least experienced because they have less at stake. The more people have at stake, the more responsibility they have, the more conservative they tend to become, and the more set in their ways.

Yet even though the young accept change more readily, they may lose that openness through a chameleon-like adapting to their surroundings.

What's been remarkable to me is how quickly some of the very people I have recruited, the very young and excited and enthusiastic, have tended to slide into set ways. You have to keep working with them, to keep tilling the earth.

Why do they do that? I think it's the way human beings manage complexity—we develop rules. This is how we reduce chaos to order. And as we do that, we automatically undermine the innovation and imagination and creativity. So there's an inherent sort of cyclical conflict between innovation, creativity, and entrepreneurship on the one hand, and reliable, scalable order on the other hand. It's an age-old conflict. The rules negate creativity, but rules are necessary.

But that's what excites me. I love the challenge of change, and I can understand why many people don't. They say, We've had enough excitement when we were teenagers, we don't need it when we are in our forties.

You have to ask them to put at risk the predictability and regularity of their business, their known quantities, in favor of something that is somewhat more amorphous, very much more uncertain, and that has a huge degree of risk from the point of view of the profitability involved.

What are some other examples revealing key cultural aspects necessary for success in the Digital Revolution? One that comes to mind was exemplified by the insurance company USAA, when it was being run in the 1970s and 1980s by CEO Robert McDermott. Here was a guy who believed that any organization, to stay fresh, had to go through a fairly aggressive reorganization at least every eighteen months. He believed that if you let things remain static for much longer, people would get too comfortable.

And there was the chairman of a large Japanese company sometime back who every three years or so would send out an announcement throughout the company, "The chairman is dead, you must now rethink the entire organization and remake it."

When change is embraced from the top, people never have a feeling that their organization, or their own position in it, will be the same two or three years down the road. They gradually come to believe that it's possible to live in a world of high uncertainty. And gradually gain the confidence that they can operate successfully in this kind of rapidly changing environment.

That's the necessary adjustment for people to become constantly open to new ideas. You have to create an environment in which people are comfortable with the idea that what they're doing today may not in fact be required to be done tomorrow, and that they may have to learn some entirely new skills.

The old high-tech industry wisdom said, Beware the company that uses technology just to let its workers do more of what they do, and do it more quickly; that means if they're making bad decisions, they then have the opportunity to make more bad decisions faster—and put the company out of business sooner.

Instead, the underlying cultural issue here is creating an environment in which people are not focused on just trying to do better what they already do, but continually looking for newer, better ways that match the needs of business in a land where e-business reigns supreme.

As companies move from a world of big-eat-small to a world of fast-eat-slow, rethinking the processes that underlie the business—the way Coles Myer does in giving stock clerks so much decision-making authority—grows in importance.

One attempt to hasten this change is seen in the creation of more "Skunk Works" projects—efforts considered so important to the company that they are given a special status, free of most of the procedural rules and bureaucratic strictures that govern the rest of the organization. (The term was, I think, made famous by Lockheed Martin Aircraft, when they gathered a special team to design and build the U-2 spy plane in the 1940s. But the term originated in, of all things, a Sunday comic strip: The *Skonk Works* was an illegal still in which a character in Al Capp's *Li'l Abner* brewed a concoction he called Kickapoo Joy Juice.)

The Skunk Works approach gets much of the credit for the success of GM's Saturn design. It was in many ways typical of the design ideas and process innovations that have come from small groups set apart from the mainstream of their organization.

Today companies need to be finding ways of taking the freedom to innovate that characterizes a Skunk Works project, and extending that freedom throughout the entire enterprise.

Other than specific instances like the Saturn, the Detroit automakers have in the past been perhaps too obviously a classic example of a major industry that just didn't get it, characterized by people at every management level who very much did not want input from anybody at a less-exalted level than their own on the organization chart.

The close-minded attitude could even be seen in the visitors' parking lot. Any idea what happened if a salesman tried to call on GM or Ford, and drove up in a car made by another company? Or, worse, a car from Germany or Japan? It was like asking to get shot in the foot.

But to me, Detroit has become a prime example of how even a behemoth of an industry is capable of shifting gears. The car companies are making an effort, and showing clear signs of progress, offering small cars and large, SUVs, and light trucks, and generally building them with higher quality than ever. And efforts like the Ford program that gives computers to employees for home use shows that the U.S. auto industry today has learned a great deal about thinking innovatively and competing effectively.

Some companies, some industries, have a greater leap to make than others. Hopefully, the distance *your* company needs to travel to reshape its culture for the e-business revolution is less intimidating than the challenge that has faced the auto companies.

One more piece of the culture change puzzle: You can't effectively reshape an organization's culture unless many of the new people you're bringing in will be effective examples and advocates of the new culture you're trying to move toward.

At Microsoft we hold very hard-core attitudes about how we hire people. Finding people who are both technically qualified and seem able to fit into our distinctive culture is a continuing challenge. A few years ago at our executive retreat, which we hold once a year, we had a discussion about this.

Out of the conversation came a commitment, one that was accepted by every executive, for himself and his entire portion of the company. The commitment said that every Microsoft employee would interview not only any finalist for a position who would report directly to them, but also anyone who was a finalist for a position working for somebody who worked for them—direct reports *plus* the second level down.

Now for many people at Microsoft, that adds up to a lot of interviewing. Yet the belief was strong that if, as we grew, we failed to maintain this focus on bringing in the right people, we would gradually lose our culture. The commitment of time we make in interviewing grows out of this inescapable sense that the culture is fundamental to the success of the company.

Not that this formulation would necessarily work for your company, but in selecting people, we look for those who will be able to function in a setting where change is the norm, where hierarchy is broken down, where people are encouraged to create ideas independent of their rank, or their age, or their education, or how long they've been with the company. Beyond the level of skills in their particular field, we want people with a passion for what they do, and people who can be comfortable in a setting of constant change— one where their group may be reorganized, or their offices moved, as frequently as every six months.

I can't close this discussion without passing along two quotes that Tony Raper shared with us as his favorites on the subject of change—quotes that, he says, he often uses with his staff.

General Raper:

> *One from Machiavelli reads, "There is no more delicate matter to take in hand, no more dangerous to conduct, no more doubtful in its success, than to set up as a leader in the introduction of change. Because the innovator has for enemies all those who have done well under the old conditions, and only lukewarm defenders in those who may do well under the new."*
>
> *The second, from Abraham Lincoln, was not necessarily meant to be used the way I use it, but it applies rather well: "The dogmas of the quiet past are inadequate for the stormy present. The occasion is piled high with difficulty and we must rise with the occasion. As our case is new, so must we think anew and act anew."*

There's a third quote, as well. This one is from the general himself.

> *If it was easy, it would not be a challenge.*

In an Internet world . . . your [methods] today can't be the same as a few years ago. We are reinventing our [methods] every month.

—David Pottruck,
CEO, Charles Schwab,
as quoted in *The New York Times*

Any sufficiently advanced technology is indistinguishable from magic.

—Arthur C. Clarke

Does Any Management Committee Really Need a Technologist?

These days, janitors call themselves "custodial engineers" and garbage collectors call themselves "sanitation workers." In that same vein, the toilers in technology departments have apparently felt that their efforts weren't respected as much as the efforts of folks whose results more directly impact the bottom line—the sales and marketing people, the product development troops, and so on.

That must explain the progression of titles that the heads of technology departments have used as they searched for a strategic meaning in life. In the early days the sign on their desks most often said something like "Manager, Data Processing."

As the work became more significant than just storing and retrieving data, that title began to sound pretty mundane, so over a period of time they finagled to have themselves redesignated as "Manager of Information Services." Eventually that no longer seemed suitable to the expanding mission and—I guess on the theory that a chief is more important than a manager—they redefined themselves once again, this time under the title of "Chief Information Officer."

More recently—I've given up imagining what the thinking process is here—they decided they should be called "Chief Knowledge Officer." That's fairly new, but some have already gone beyond, becoming a CIO again—except on this go-around, it now stands for "Chief Innovation Officer."

Will having that title help people be more innovative? More effective? More strategic minded? We can only hope so. After a while you begin to wonder if some of these people are too worried about their title to be focusing on how they can make the best contribution to their organizations.

Information Technology has historically had the role of managing the technical infrastructure of the company and responding to the business organization's demand for technical support—making sure the phones ring, keeping the software updated and running, buying the computers and laptops, and, more recently, seeing that the Web site doesn't get overloaded, worrying about firewalls and security, and the rest.

As we've mentioned, a debate is raging over whether the technology manager's role should change beyond merely managing the plumbing to some more strategic role. Traditionally, the technology group has reported either to the COO/vice president of administration or the CFO/vice president of finance, or someone else at this level.

Many companies these days have figured out that Information Technology does indeed have a more strategic role than just some internal support function.

But the debate isn't new—it's been argued for as long as I've been in data processing, which means at least thirty years.

It's time to put the debate behind us. As I maintain throughout these pages, technology has become a catalyst for changing the very business you are in. Because of that, the person responsible for managing the organization's technology clearly has a strategic role to play.

This doesn't imply that technology chiefs make the business case for technology. I believe that's a grave mistake. But—the main point here—because he or she is the most knowledgeable person about the technology, the technology leader must take on an expanded role in the organization, must provide guidance, and thought leadership, to the other executives on technology's impact on strategy.

There's only one way for this to be effective—

> **The technology leader must become a member of the most senior executive team of the organization. He or she must be able to speak to the other top executives, not as an adviser, but as a peer.**

(There are cases, of course, where another senior executive with the appropriate experience is able to represent IT issues at the executive table, so that there is less need for having the technology boss included.)

With this new role comes a heavy burden of responsibility—

> **The technology leader must move up his or her level of responsibilities by understanding much more about the business than in the past.**

Archie Kane of Lloyds TSB has recently been made a member of the bank's highest executive group. We wondered how a British bank—not usually thought of as pacesetters in management—came to be so far in front on this.

Archie Kane:
> I think it's happened because there has been a realization at the highest levels of the importance of technology. Now that's fine to say; how did it come about?

When I took over IT and Operations, one of the things I started was to have a once-a-year major presentation to the board—a two- to three-hour presentation. This was not a classic technology report full of lots of stuff about "These are our technology platforms, this is the number of MIPs we have, this is the number of transactions we're doing," and so on. We covered that, but with one slide in amongst sixty.

What we said instead was, "These are the key areas for the business, these are the key deliverables we're involved in, these are the key issues that this business needs to grapple with in the world of technology." For example, integrating our business systems, but from a business perspective, and what are we going to deliver that will help the customer, and help the staff interface with the customer? What are we doing in the areas of e-commerce and the Internet?

So I turned the whole thing around and presented the entire report from a business perspective, with all of the backup of the IT details if they wished to delve into the appendixes.

And I believe those presentations were hugely instrumental in bringing the board and top management of the company forward, in terms of really grasping the importance that technology had to play in the business. I think that played a part in the idea of having someone with a technology background on the Executive Committee.

A lot of people throughout the business world are as dependent on technology and what their IT people are doing as Archie Kane was, but don't come out of that experience qualified to take on a technology role in their companies. What was the secret?

I've had the view for some time that if you're going to run a business in the future, technology has to be viewed as a core competence, in the same way that you would have with marketing or finance.

The CEOs of the future will need to have a very good grasp of what technology can do for them and what the key risks and key issues are in technology. I think at the highest levels in companies, people are going to have to be technology literate.

.   .   .

Texaco stands out as a company that has also seen the wisdom of this philosophy.

Ed McDonald:

The top technology officer of Texaco is on the Executive Committee—the only member who is not a senior vice president of an operating division.

The relationship between Information Technology and the senior leadership of the corporation at Texaco goes way back. Our first CIO recommended that a separate department be formed, and the first head of this new department—the Computer Services Department, it was called at the time—was a fellow who had been VP of refining. He was the first technology leader of Texaco, his role was to act as the bridge to the businesses, and he had a working relationship with the chairman.

The problem is that during some period we lost a close working relationship with the middle management, the folks that were running individual business units. The company changed its organization from a highly centralized structure run from headquarters, to a distributed organization. In the formation of strategic business units, the relationship was not as tight between these younger folks who were being put into general management roles and their technology staff people.

So the field technology people had good ties back to headquarters, but didn't have as close ties as they needed with their own operating units in the field.

We've strengthened that now. The organization that was the Information Strategy Group has been turned into a governing board that actually controls the budgets and approves the plans of the Information Technology Group. It's in fact become the equivalent of a board of directors.

So we've reestablished that close working relationship with middle management now, actually even made it stronger.

The secretary of technology for the state of Virginia has a different way of describing the challenge.

Don Upson:

> *The head of technology for any organization has to be more than just a per-*
> *son who orders computers and keeps them running. The person has to*
> *understand the enterprise.*
>
> *That means challenge—challenge the rules, challenge the bureaucracy,*
> *whether it's a company or a country. The world is not changing, it has*
> *already changed, and we haven't kept up with it.*
>
> *Those organizations that manage to catch on will be around; those that*
> *don't, won't. If you continue to do things the way you've always done them*
> *without challenging them all the time, you'll end up out of business.*

At Scottish Power, David Jones has "overall group responsibility for how IT enables and helps the businesses drive forward." Wearing another hat, he's also managing director of the Information Systems Division, an internal organization that operates like a commercial concern, doing business outside the company. The transition in the role of a CIO that we've been discussing was something that David has had the opportunity of seeing at close hand: it happened to him. There was a point when the executive management of the company recognized that the head of technology had to be more than just the person running the technology group—he had to be taking a strategic role in the decisions that the company was making.

David Jones:

> *It was two to three years of earning my spurs, of demonstrating that I could*
> *deliver the IT enablement the business wanted. That then established the*
> *relationship with the executive directors.*
>
> *I used that relationship to talk to them about what the future opportuni-*
> *ties and threats were. So it was a combination of being able to deliver what*
> *they needed today and to show them the advantage of what they could do*
> *tomorrow. The combination got the message over that, Yes, maybe there is*
> *value in having this individual as part of our strategic discussions. They*
> *decided, "The manager of the team has some good views of what the future*

could look like and what the technology could do for the company, and so it's important that he be part of the overall management team."

The CIO was made a member of the Executive Management Team of the company in 1997.

I was surprised, delighted, more important, I think, proud for the whole team that what we had done had been recognized as being now of a strategic value to the organization.

But Microsoft's sales and marketing VP Jeff Raikes thinks the change in the role of the CIO might be even more radical.

Jeff Raikes:

The corporate structure was set up where you've got person A running division A, and person B running division B, and then you have a corporate staff position called the CIO that's supposed to do the technology for all these businesses.

I think in a certain sense that represents old-world thinking where technology was more of an adjunct as opposed to being at the heart of how the business is run—to the point where person A and person B didn't need to know about the technology because of the corporate CIO.

Today technology is so much a part of everything we do. I sometimes wonder whether the CIO position will even exist in the future.

If technology is to take on a new role of helping to set the strategic goals of a company, does the leader of the technology organization need to be a businessperson instead of someone with a technology background?

People who've spent all their lives in technology come to have quite a struggle when they move out of the technology arena into the world of top management. In my experience a lot of technology people—not all of them, but a lot of them—struggle with that.

If CIOs are going to fulfill the potential that they should fulfill, then they're going to have to become more well rounded at an earlier stage in their career.

And if that's the case, then you can no longer say that the people who are going to succeed and drive your company are the great people managers or the great deal makers or the great marketers, and ignore their ability to use technology for creating competitive advantage. It's entirely illogical that you would fail to include the application of technology in a set of core competencies.

When I deliver a speech about this, people come up afterward and say, "Yeah, you're absolutely right." But when I ask, "Tell me how you do it in your company or your business area," they shrug and come back with views not very well thought out.

To my mind, spending time in and around technology is going to be one of those key things a manager will need in order to rise to the executive level. That's not an entirely novel idea, of course; forward-looking executives have been expressing similar ideas for some time. For example—

Archie Kane:

> Managers need to understand how they can deploy and use technology, how it will help them reduce the cost, increase sales, and increase customer service and satisfaction.
>
> Once they start to get a handle on those things, then they start to attack the technology issue, the great magic box if you like, in a more sensible way. They start to unpack it, break it down into modular bits that fit in customer end-to-end processes, all the way through to customer satisfaction. And they start to see that technology plays a part in not only the sales process but the customer service process.
>
> So once you start to explain it in those terms, I think people start to sud-

denly see, Hey, yes, technology is a part of the kit bag that I need to assemble in my development as a manager.

Although not many are running to it right now, I think we will find more and more people preparing themselves like that.

An excellent reminder on equipping yourself for executive management.

CHAPTER 12

In the Internet environment, change is valued more than stability. E-business is based on a solid faith in continuous beginnings.

—PRICE PRITCHETT

Using Technology to Blow Up Your Processes

Technology can be a light in the dark that leads you to question how you could make dramatic improvements in some of your long-established business processes. More than that, technology can lead you to question whether some of these processes are needed at all.

You can use technology to "blow up" processes that have been in place for years and years.

If you look at the history of computing, it has been for the most part focused on letting us be more efficient. I gave examples earlier about airline reservations systems, about accounting systems, and so on. At the dawn of the Digital Revolution/e-business age, if you limit yourself to a continuation of business process reengineering, you miss the opportunity—the *necessity*—to totally rethink your processes.

Imagine, for example, if the management of your company goes to the head of Purchasing and says, "We're bringing in some new technology that will make your operations more efficient." Fine— happens every day, nobody sweats it. But when the head of Purchasing, or any other department or operation, instead hears, "We're bringing in some new technology that will blow up your processes and probably do away with a whole lot of what you do"— now that's got to be threatening to any manager or leader.

Yet it's essential.

I sometimes talk about what I call the crystal-radio environment. The crystal radio was a gadget, in a sense hardly more than a toy, that proto-nerds in the early part of the 1900s, in the earliest days of radio broadcasting, fiddled with in hopes of picking up an audible radio signal out of the ether. It was made up of a battery, a thin pigtail of wire on a pivot, a pair of earphones, and a small, glistening piece of piezoelectric crystal. The user pivoted the pigtail to touch its point against the crystal, trying over and over until, if he were lucky, he would eventually pluck a radio signal out of the ether— barely audible, but nonetheless real. A thrilling moment.

Before television, before radio, even before the crystal radio, back to Homer, back further to the earliest tribal storytellers, there have always been people who had something to say, a story to tell, a voice they wanted to exercise. And there have always been people with an ear for more than just listening—to comprehend, translate, and do something as a result of the stories.

For centuries the only way the connection took place was when the storyteller and the listener were in each other's presence. Radio brought a phenomenal change to that by putting broadcasters and receivers who never would have been in touch, into contact with each other. And it transformed one-on-one communications to one-to-the-thousands, one-to-the-millions.

The crystal radio, with the telephone that preceded it, were technologies that blew up the centuries-old communications paradigm. If you had said then that you were comfortable with the old ways and didn't want the new, you would have been slamming the doors and condemning your company.

The Internet has brought another crystal-radio experience, but it adds the crucial, incredibly powerful element of interactivity that creates an incredibly powerful new context. It brings the opportunity not just to extract, not just to listen, but to *collaborate*—to truly create new intellectual capital.

When I sit down with a CEO and talk about a business transformation in the corporation, what I tell him is, "Look, you don't just want to sell your customer more products over the Internet, you want your customer to come back and tell you new features that you should be putting in your products, new features you should be adding to your services." In the same way, you want to go back to your customers and tell them, "Hey, I'm adding this functionality that can be valuable to you." And through this dialogue, you can stimulate each other to higher and better utilization of your products and services, and create new ideas.

Mike Turillo of KPMG, who holds the title of global knowledge officer, works in what he refers to as "the visionary side of the house," regularly moving new ideas from concept to reality. The problem that his company faced in 1998 was one that will sound familiar to many.

Mike Turillo:

> Until recently most KPMG people didn't know their own organization. By this I mean that few within our organization had any idea where to turn for any particular expertise. And with 110,000 employees worldwide, one can only imagine how many "individual" areas of expertise remained hidden. Not terribly impressive for a knowledge-based company!
>
> Like most organizations, we had pockets of expertise and over time had built up personal networks—I know you, you know me, because we worked together five years ago on a project. But it could take us days or weeks to find out what we had done to solve a problem in the past that could be applied to a new situation. It was very frustrating and not at all efficient.

This need for worldwide connectivity is something new for us. Not that long ago, we could serve our clients almost entirely with local resources. A small research staff at the local office could gather most of the information needed and a project team could be built on the back of a personal Rolodex.

But in today's Internet-driven world, even our regionally based clients demand advisers with national and global perspectives.

To meet these changing needs, and to become a more effective and efficient knowledge-sharing culture, KPMG created a Web-based interface they dubbed "KWorld."

Today's environment demands collaboration. Through KWorld, KPMG professionals can draw upon the full range of our intellectual assets.

We knew that we had to become a truly global firm, focused very much on certain products and services against certain market areas. And we needed to maximize the intellectual capital that we had by being the best in the marketplace.

The transition to KWorld meant a departure from traditional vendor-client relationships. It also meant revisiting the agility, responsiveness, and connectivity that a smaller firm or start-up is often viewed as being better at. When you become large, the "dis" words have a tendency to take over: disjointed, disconnected, dysfunctional.

And if looking in the mirror wasn't enough of a catalyst for change, we also had an external event that shocked our system and bolted us out of complacency. Merger discussions with another major firm forced us to re-examine our organization and re-assess our business priorities moving forward. While a major shift in thinking at KPMG was already in the works, talk of a merger expedited development of KWorld.

Some of the benefits were unexpected. For example—

We had been spending $20 to 30 million annually purchasing subscriptions to news sources. I was able to reduce that number by more than 60 percent by eliminating redundancy, duplication, and inefficiency. So it's not that *we've just bought less, we've bought smarter. We're buying world-class data and we're disseminating it more efficiently.*

Another invaluable benefit was the greatly reduced turnaround time for learning specifics about past KPMG accomplishments. What used to take days or weeks now happens in minutes by interrogating the KWorld environment.

As a result of this new environment and being able to overcome our technology angst, we have thousands of people comprising hundreds of teams that can draw on the full range of our firm's intellectual assets—through a unique search mechanism that we designed to parallel our way of doing business.

Using KWorld, our people are able to access the right information at the right time, in essence allowing us to leapfrog our competition.

And what lessons can be drawn from the KPMG experience to guide others? Mike Turillo has a ready answer.

If I had to summarize in one word, it's collaboration.

To successfully move forward, a company must figure out how to get the best out of itself and its people. For KPMG, the strategy was to develop a process that enabled its 110,000 employees and professionals to document all ideas and accomplishments in a readily accessible knowledge base. Such a knowledge-sharing environment would allow us to think and act in a clearer, more resourceful, and more constructive way.

These thoughts are underscored by the chairman of KPMG.

Colin Sharman:

We believe that knowledge resides with the practitioner and professional who has to deal with the expert in the field, not with some crew of people from the back office. Success or failure often depends upon getting the right information to the right person at exactly the right time.

Through the application of technology, KWorld provides an essential cutting-edge environment which will change the way we do business. It's the

key to helping each of us increase our efficiency and as well making the
knowledge of the global firm work for the benefit of our clients.
  It's a crucial component to achieving our firm's global goals.

A prime example of using the power of technology to blow up outmoded processes.

This transition that KPMG so recently went through has been going on at Microsoft for years, very much because of the management style of Bill Gates and, more recently, Steve Ballmer. A prime example is the story of the Microsoft Procurement Department.

We don't view the Procurement process any differently than you do. We probably don't do HR a lot differently, we probably don't do payroll a lot differently. Every company can convince itself it does all these things differently than anyone else, and it's nonsense—we all do these processes essentially same way.

At Microsoft until five or six years ago we had a situation where every employee was a Procurement agent—they had a phone and the Yellow Pages. Our COO tells the story.

Bob Herbold:
  We would get bills from vendors that we had never even heard of and we
  hadn't the faintest idea why we owed them money or whether we really did
  owe them money. It was a real mess.

  Of course, that's human nature. Left unbridled, that's the way humans
  like to operate. So a CIO has somewhat of the whole world working against
  him or her, and the only way out of that mess is discipline and standards,
  plus being hard nosed and having a lot of backbone. And it helps to have
  your CEO behind you as you stand tall saying to all these people, Now we're
  going do it this new, standard way.

  We said to the Procurement people, Who are the people and organiza-
  tions that are ordering paper forms? And they listed all the forms that were

*used by all these different departments and organizations. The objective
was to eliminate all of them.*

Before a company can start eliminating paper forms and putting
templates on line, there's an essential preliminary step.

*Step one, and this is important, is for a company to fix its network infrastruc-
ture so that everybody can get at information electronically. And secondly,
they have to worry about what devices are they going to authorize and stan-
dardize on so all employees can get at information via that network. That's
the basic plumbing, and naturally that's where you need to start.*

   *To some extent, we had a leg up over other organizations. We already had
an internal network and were using e-mail as the tool for communications,
and naturally we standardized on up-to-date PCs running Windows software.*

So we got rid of the forms. Finally somebody said, "Hey, wait a
minute, maybe it's not just getting rid of forms, maybe there are a
lot of procedures here we could get rid of, as well."

The question then became, What are the processes we really need
to be doing here to maintain appropriate, fiscally responsible controls, and what are the processes we could just plain get rid of?

*What people are often reluctant to do is to grab that paper form and say, first
of all the paper form is gone. Secondly, the people who used to handle the
paper form are gone. Thirdly, the people who used to answer questions
about how to fill out the paper form are gone.*

   *It's important to eliminate all those people because otherwise the sav-
ings aren't there.*

In the end we devised a new set of rules and procedures for how
employees would do their requisitioning and buying; importantly,
it was paperless, and it was based on off-the-shelf software and
friendly, Web-based menus. No systems development of the tradi-

tional type was required. We created new software for the purpose—that's the technology part—and then we ran the new system in parallel with the old one, just the way you're supposed to do, until the bugs were worked out and the concept was proven.

Then we all but shut down the old system and we told our employees everywhere on Earth, If you want to order a pencil, a personal computer, anything at all, don't call Procurement—the old phone number won't even be answered. No busy signal, no voice mail message, it's a dead phone number. No one's there, so don't bother to call. The catalog of everything you can order is online, and it's the only way you'll be able to get what you want.

Another example of using technology to sweep away a process that didn't make sense. What did it bring us? Methods for buying that improve productivity by sweeping away a great deal of paperwork, that allow order placing twenty-four hours a day, seven days a week, and that do away with a lot of unnecessary paper-pushing jobs.

Yes, a system like this calls for good judgment and 100 percent compliance on the part of your employees. And, yes, there will always be the occasional person who abuses the privileges. But managers track what their employees have purchased. And anyone who betrays trust by abusing the privilege isn't around long enough to do it a second time.

Meanwhile, what happened to all the people we didn't need in Procurement any more? At Microsoft, our view is that if the world were a perfect place, every single employee in this company would do either of two things: deal with our customers, or build great products.

So we offered retraining opportunities, aiming to let the ex-Procurement people contribute to the company in other areas. We're always looking for more good people; the last thing we want to do is let good people go.

In the end we reduced the Procurement expenses of Microsoft Corporation by 70 percent. Let me do that again: not 7 percent, but *70*. I think you'll agree that's a big number.

When I give talks on this, I end by saying, "People ask me why this isn't being changed in every company. And I answer that there are five reasons." And then I give the list I cited earlier: politics, stupidity, bureaucracy, turf battles, and inertia.

Bill Gates himself described all this at one of our gatherings for CEOs, and something like half the executives present went back to their offices and told their CIOs, "I heard about this new Procurement approach, we need to be doing this."

Overhauling your processes for the needs of the Digital Age is—I trust this is obvious—not a one-shot deal. There are no permanent solutions; once changed, the new processes can't be carved in stone. Microsoft's COO considers maintaining the ability to change your processes over time as "critically important."

Bob Herbold:

You leave that up to the small group of experts that in fact are running each process and are responsible for keeping it up to date.

But if you simplify each of those core processes in the company and simplify the systems, your ability to change is very high. That small group of people in charge of the small number of key systems that are used globally can integrate changes quickly.

If you've simplified the processes, then changes, when needed, are vastly more straightforward.

It's all very simple compared to the complicated web that human beings always get themselves involved with when they're allowed to argue that their needs are different and they have to have special systems and the like. If you've given in to those arguments, then when you try and change something, you have to get in there and figure out all those connections, which can take months and months and months.

These are guidelines I always salute. But once again the secret is support from the top management. When that cranky senior vice president, who is the favorite of the CEO, knocks on the CEO's door and wants those exceptions, the CEO knows well enough that it's going to cost him an arm and a leg if he allows that disease to creep in. And so he says, "No, go see the person who's in charge of that process"—knowing full well that person won't allow any exceptions.

Microsoft, of course, doesn't have an exclusive when it comes to the subject of applying technology to rethinking purchasing processes. The concatenation of Ford, GM, and DaimlerChrysler I mentioned earlier is a near unbeatable example of replacing old thinking with new, by applying technology.

In the usual auto industry way of doing things, Ford would have optimized its purchasing scheme, GM would have tackled the same problem and come up with a different solution, and ditto DaimlerChrysler. The significant element in the story? That *technology* was the driving force which led to the tripartite solution that holds the potential of incredible money-saving, effort-saving results.

There's a big consulting industry built up around the idea of business process reengineering (BPR), originated by Michael Hammer and James Champy. And I'm not suggesting great things didn't happen there; certainly a lot of processes were improved. But in the current climate, limiting your efforts to attempts at improving existing processes limits the potential for realizing the payoff of technology.

And my view is that if you are not focused on looking at the possibility of revamping or discarding processes that may be outmoded or entirely unnecessary, some competitor is going to figure it out and leave you looking like you're standing still.

The heart of the message is extending the view beyond just making your company more efficient at doing the things you're already doing.

You heard the voice of Major General Tony Raper in a previous chapter, so it won't surprise you any to learn that he, too, is finding ways to blow up outmoded processes.

General Raper:

What we have tended to do is, like most organizations, we've handled infor-mation in a hierarchical way . . . vertically up and down the chain with no short circuits.

But it doesn't always have to work like that. General Raper called on his knowledge of military history to offer an example that sounds very much like one of the beginnings—from a surprising source—for the current speedup in information.

If you go back to Napoleonic times, Napoleon tried to short-circuit the tradi-tional information flow with a technique he referred to as his "directed tele-scope." He knew there was going to be information that would take time to get to him, information which was crucial—whether it be information that enabled him to gain some advantage over his opponent, or whether it be information that was reporting an adverse situation.

The "telescope"—in reality his liaison officers—enabled him to get infor-mation quicker and react to it sooner. He recognized a need to move infor-mation outside of the hierarchical structure.

Most hierarchical organizations, General Raper points out, are not comfortable with short-circuiting the information flow.

Web technology today makes information readily available to everyone in a way that simply couldn't be accessed before. We have to look at what that actually means for our modus operandi *as well as our organizational structures.*

For the military, it affects how we deploy. You may no longer need to deploy everything to an operational theater that you used to. The reason is that if you can make the information available instantly on what supplies you're using and what you're going to need, then you can initially deploy perhaps only a third of the resources you would have before. This is what might be called battlefield just-in-time logistics.

In the intelligence arena, you are better now at enabling information to be pulled directly by the operational commanders.

I would like to see us exploiting more in terms of getting a much better handle on the rate at which we're consuming resources and where we're consuming resources in an operational theater—as opposed to what we have tended to do in the past, which is quite simply to overstock because we haven't had the means of making consumption levels instantly visible.

Another favorite example of using technology to blow up processes: the case of the Snapper Power Equipment Company, of McDonough, Georgia. Here was a firm about as traditional as you could find, nearly fifty years old, selling very-high-quality lawn care equipment—lawn mowers, weed eaters, and so on.

The company had a conventional value chain—factory to distributors, to retailers, to the customer—operating with a small group of salespeople, about thirty distributors, and thousands of retailers. A good business, with a strong, respected brand name and good, healthy margins.

All of a sudden along comes the Internet and within a couple of years Snapper is facing online auctions where customers bid how much they want to pay for a lawn mower. Suddenly, cutthroat discount operations are coming in from the left and the right; overnight, Snapper's margins are under pressure. The company is forced to rethink whether it really needs certain pieces of that value chain—in particular, the distributors.

Snapper ended up bypassing all the distributors; instead, it increased its internal sales force from about five people to about eighty-five, who now were dealing directly with the retailers.

That sounded like a good solution, but the salespeople were soon drowning in paperwork. Their paper-based sales and order systems, which were fine for thirty distributor customers, choked when the customer base suddenly numbered in the thousands, from mom-and-pop stores to the Home Depot chain. Sales representatives were lugging heavy catalogs and price books into dozens of dealer show-rooms and racing to record orders on paper forms and fax them back.

The situation became so bad that, as one company executive described it, "We were not getting orders into the factory or product out of the factory in time, we were getting the wrong orders, we were dropping orders. Dealers didn't have what they needed from us, so they were selling somebody else's product. Lawn mowers are all about floor space: If it's not there on the floor, you can't sell it. We were losing money."

At that point the company turned to an outside technology consulting firm, which recommended a sales force automation system.

Once it was up and running, Snapper found it had rid itself of a bundle of costs; but that was by no means the most interesting part of the story. The company discovered that where in the past the factory told the distributors what to sell, now they found the retailers were telling the plant what the customers would buy. In effect, they had opened a channel for the customers to tell the company what the Snapper products should be like.

I think that's a wonderful way to describe the impact you want to have—blowing up a process and gaining more direct input, more immediate communication, with the customers becoming a driving force in product design. It doesn't get better than that.

Few people expect to find an example of management leadership in an "old economy" company, certainly not a company in an industry as old, as traditional, as electric utilities. And even less likely in cold, out-of-the-way Scotland. But the interview earlier in these pages revealed Scottish Power as refuting all the clichéd assumptions. The company's group chief information officer described for us how "blowing up the processes" can sometimes be easier for a person brought in from the outside.

David Jones:

When I was being interviewed for this position, one of the first questions asked me by the chairman was, "Mr. Jones, what are you going to do about the fact that you know nothing about the utilities industry." And I said, "Mr. Chairman, I see that as an asset, not a liability."

I think one of the reasons I was hired was that they saw I could bring a different mindset to the way the business could go forward. It's an asset not to know the industry. You tend to ask very dumb questions; nine times out of ten there's a good answer, but it's the one out of ten where you ask about a process and somebody says, "That's actually a very good question— nobody seems to ask why we do it that way." Whereas somebody who's been embroiled in the work just doesn't ask the dumb questions.

And not just with processes. I believe that if you come from outside an industry, you can give a vision of other things that can be done with consumers, as well.

As a company like Scottish Power extends its line of products and services, it will grow its customer relationship. At the moment, the mindset in much of the utility industry holds that products and services, and customer relationships, are the same category of thing, and they're all run by the same operating division.

That simply doesn't work in the technology future. It really doesn't work. I think I've got the message across that IT is there as an enabler, it's there not just to help the business today, but it's also a strategic asset that can very much help the business for tomorrow. It's all about a partnership between IT and the business. And given the right partnership, what you have is a very strong future business strategy underwritten by an enabling IT strategy.

In Australia, Coles Myer's Dennis Eck complains of a roadblock that stands in the way of effective change for many companies. Speaking of his ideas about feeding information upward instead of downward, he says, "In my experience, ideas like this make academics particularly mad." As he sees the world—

Most management theory is a ready-to-wear suit. It's better than being naked but it doesn't quite fit you. In today's environment, technology allows you to tailor the way you manage a business.

Dennis Eck's view is that "anybody who doesn't use technology that way is not getting enough out of their technology." He also strongly believes that—

The further impact of technology is that the amount of time you can be ordinary today has shortened.

And what, in this context, does Dennis mean by *ordinary*?

I mean not focused, not providing a high-quality experience for your suppliers, your employees, or your customers. If you're ordinary today, somebody can very quickly (a) recognize it, and (b) quickly move in and make an offer that puts you under incredible strain.

And Dennis reiterates his notion about the direction of data flow.

The main thing we learn about the computer today is that it's pointed in the wrong direction. It's been pointed inward, controlling and massaging data; it should be pointed outward, distributing knowledge back to the center.

.   .   .

Today we score ourselves high if we're using technology effectively. Tomorrow we'll score ourselves high only if we're using technology to knock out unnecessary procedures, blow them up, and, in many cases, discover we haven't needed them for years.

Some companies, as we've seen, are already showing the way.

*The Information Technology group must become
more than just a part of the cost solution,
it must become part of the business solution.*

—GARY MOORE, CEO, NETIGY

You Can't Lead
Unless You Bleed

"Technology has changed, film at eleven." That could be the television news teaser . . . every day.

It won't come as any surprise to hear that technology is changing faster than ever, at an increasingly rapid pace. And yet, it's still fairly common for a business to look at investing in information technology with a view that says, "Let some others try it, get all the problems fixed, then we'll jump in—we may have missed a few months, even a year, but that won't impact the business in a strategic way. Better to let someone else take the risk."

I argue that you have to get on the bleeding edge. At least a little. If you don't, you run the substantial danger of somebody getting a jump-start that may leave you in the dust, struggling to see your way.

The wait and see approach may have worked in the past, but will not work in the future. Sure, you'll make some mistakes by being on the forefront . . . but at far less cost than being left behind.

My message to company leaders for years has been, "Don't worry about the technology, focus on how you basically do things differently and better. The technology will be there."

What I offer here is not tactical formulas for adopting technology, but inspiration and strategic visions from individuals and companies that, in my view, have the right attitude and approach, the guts, the foresight, and the initiative to be ahead of the pack: on the bleeding edge.

As should be clear from earlier in these pages, Texaco shines as an example of a company that has long been willing to be on the cutting edge of technology. The firm's Ed McDonald has observed this evolution from what now seem like primitive times, starting even before he joined the company.

Ed McDonald:

> When I was a graduate student at Rice, the computer I had available was at Texas A&M University, about sixty miles up the road. I would punch up a card deck, take it to the Greyhound bus station, put it on a bus. It would arrive at Texas A&M, they would run it through the compiler, then drive it back to the bus station and send it off. I'd go down to the station at six in the morning and pick up the results.

After starting his career with Texaco, Ed saw the company innovating with technology—though some of the examples seem laughable now.

> We had a remote card reader at our refinery in Convent, Louisiana, four hundred miles away from our data center in Houston. They would take a card deck and put the data into the card reader and send it across the telephone line.
>
> On a computer at the data center, an optimization program would be run to tell them how to change the operation of the plant in Louisiana. Then the data would be sent back, and the people in Louisiana would make correc-

tions to their process-control computer to change how the refining process was running.

What is it that gives one company the culture and the ability to march at the bleeding edge of change, when other companies are waiting for some consultant or vendor to come along and say, "Here's an idea, a product, a capability, that a lot of other companies have started to use"?

Texaco's McDonald has a ready answer. "An enterprise is made up of a series of conversations." The ability to move and change, he believes, depends on the extent that a company is open to new conversations. "That is to say, they're not ossified, they don't have a strong absolute chain of command, 'This is the way we've always done it here' and 'You have to ask permission.' " Attitudes like that, in Ed's view, are the killers.

Calling on a now-familiar adage, he says, "Very early on I found the attitude at Texaco was that it's easier to ask for forgiveness than it is for permission." The view was, If it looks like there's some better way to do something, try it; if it works, tell others about it. Then if someone still says, "That's not the way we do it here," Ed's approach was to reply, "Well, I'm sorry, I didn't understand that, but look here, this other way works better and costs less money, why don't we try it like this?"

What it takes most of all is an atmosphere of trust and an openness to innovation. Even in organizations with a traditional hierarchical structure, there are pockets of innovation. Foster them—the spirit of innovation can spread like wildfire.

Earlier we described the time when Microsoft pulled together all of its various procurement groups and procedures, installed standardized procedures, and formed a small corporate department that was put in charge of the core process. What followed was an example of "bleeding edge" in a different sense: recognizing that a big change in using technology doesn't have to require a massive effort.

Bob Herbold:

> *Once we had cleaned up the procurement process, the rest became easy. We decided to create a Web-based procurement system for our employees. It was done by a group of five people who put the new system in place in five months.*
>
> *And today that system, which is used in forty-six countries, has one and a half people supporting it, because it's brutally simple — it's nothing but Web pages connected to "packaged software" procurement modules. And you can change Web pages in hours.*
>
> *Consequently by following this idea, if you make a change in the business process, you just have to change Web pages. You have gained the ability to be so agile in terms of dealing with new business designs and the like.*

For some companies, recognition of the need to move quickly to the bleeding edge of technology strikes like a bolt of lightning. Merrill Lynch first vice president Tony Pizi saw his company get that kind of sudden wake-up call. "I think the fact that the company was viewed as anti-Internet, because of some misunderstood statements by our vice chairman, was affecting our value. When Schwab passed us in market cap, that was a profound event for senior managers who are charged with increasing shareholder value. That was no small thing."

Tony was fascinated to watch the positions of senior management evolve. For years, self-service had been looked down on as the low end of the financial business. Tony tried to make executives understand how the world was changing by asking, "Would you bank at any financial institution that wasn't part of an ATM network?"

Merrill Lynch has some fifteen thousand of what Pizi refers to as "highly trained, highly skilled knowledge workers" who have built trust relationships with their mostly affluent customers. The challenge, he says, was "to morph these contacts into much more substantive relationships."

The changeover to full e-business strategy is rarely easy.

> *I wouldn't want to trivialize the changes that we had to go through. When you operate domestically, you could have a window of time where you do nightly processing. Globalization and 7×24, in particular, required profound changes. So we were affected in very fundamental ways by the Internet.*

Still, the struggle has been clearly worth it. Merrill Lynch is now fully competitive for customers who want to review their positions or do all their trading online. Yet there's no relaxing. In Pizi's vivid description—

> **The rich collaborative spaces lie ahead. The profound opportunities of technology are still in front of us.**

For another financial firm, the wake-up call sounded in a different way. At Credit Suisse First Boston, one of the co–chief information officers describes how it happened.

Steve Long:

> *There was a debt offering by a big customer, but they said they would not accept phone bids any longer, they would accept bids only from banks that could participate electronically. We didn't have any way of doing this, so we had to write software in about two weeks in order to participate.*
>
> *I think that was the wake-up call that technology was not optional. It was quite a sea change. There will be more and more examples of this for the bank over the next year and beyond, more and more pushes and requirements to be completely electronic.*

Partly growing out of this experience, the firm has recently formed a new division called CSFB*Next.*

Formerly, e-commerce has been splintered among several groups. CSFBNext becomes our institutional e-commerce effort—a single effort for the whole firm. This gives our customers one Web interface to deal with all our products.

The division contains its own e-technology group, which is part of my IT world, and has some of our best people in it. They sit with a business group, forming what's like a company within a company. It's going to be the vehicle for delivering the full range of our products to our customers via the Internet.

In today's world of smaller government budgets, the pressure for using technology in innovative ways is a challenge for military organizations as well as industry.

General Raper:

We are now beginning to see what I would call enlightened top-down direction. The new Defence Logistic Organisation has been presented with a strategic challenge by its first chief, General Sir Sam Cowan, to reduce its output cost by 20 percent in resource terms over the next five years and in the process remove much of the risk.

It's not a case of just trying to function more efficiently; clearly this requires a fundamentally different approach, one that is output focused and performance driven—and hence information enabled. The change program is recognized as the largest corporate change program in the U.K. If we are to achieve the goals, we've now got to exploit technology, exploit e-commerce and e-procurement.

With his Communication Services Agency now part of the newly created Logistics Organisation, General Raper is tackling the problem using an unexpected approach.

We're starting to challenge the boundaries governing the involvement of industry in the support of military capability. The more that we can involve industry, the more we can release resources for frontline service.

We're seeking to deliver 150 percent of what they were doing, but deliver it for 120 percent of the cost.

The biggest challenge, believe it or not, comes down to the one of owner-ship. What we've had until now is that each area has tended to own its own system, control the people who deliver it, and so on. What we're trying to do is get the organizations in U.K. Defence to recognize that the information infrastructure should merely be delivered to them as a service whenever pos-sible and that they should be focusing on their business processes, rather than concerning themselves with the delivery of the infrastructure.

Sound like a familiar problem?

So the issue is how to get people to accept that someone else can deliver to you what Bill Gates refers to as the digital nervous system. And I would have to tell you that this is extremely difficult. But we have made huge progress here, whereby people have now recognized that this is the way we must go if we are to be able to exploit information in the way that we need to for opera-tional and business purposes.

One of the arresting aspects of the e-business age: the way that the Internet provides easy access to unexpected markets. Applied Indus-trial Technologies, a Cleveland distributor of bearings, motors, and other industrial parts, uses its Internet site for reaching out directly to farmers. As reported by the *Cincinnati Enquirer*, the company in the past has found it difficult to reach these customers, but are now "tapping into the increasing level of computer sophistication down on the farm."

For today's farmers, "ordering parts over the Internet should be a snap," the article noted, since many "already have combines equipped with laptops, attend online auctions and use computers to check prices on the Chicago Board of Trade." Farmers driving combines equipped with laptops—what a great symbol of the Dig-ital Age!

The company is finding another advantage, as well: Increasing sales over the Web is allowing them "to free up people to work on more profitable projects." The company's CEO told the reporter, Thomas W. Gerdel, "We could use that manpower to do more of a technological sell and support the higher end of our selling."

"If you look at the Industrial Revolution, what you find is that it was an extension of the human body. If you look at the technology revolution, what you find is that it's the extension of the human mind. The jobs of the future are going to be between two ears. We're absolutely convinced on our campus that we expand and enhance that intellect through the use of technology." The speaker is Longwood College president Dr. Patricia Cormier.

The school's view of the importance of mastering technology has led to a thorough rethinking of how learning is imparted, as well as the requirements for being considered "educated."

Dr. Cormier:

> We have a laptop requirement for every incoming freshman, and you can't graduate from the institution without having basic skills in technology, which include everything from the obvious—word processing, e-mail, and the Internet—to spreadsheets and PowerPoint presentations, as well as technology skills specific to the student's major.
>
> My classrooms are now wired for direct access into the Internet. Students come in and plug in their laptop computers. The professor says, "Okay, let's look at some of the database related to economic development in the Sahara." The students are able, right there in the classroom, to maneuver through the database he has presented, and to look up information on the Internet.
>
> They're looking at things in almost real time that in the past they'd have to go back to a library to look up. They can actually do it right in the classroom with the professor in front of them.
>
> And there's this incredible access that students now have—24 hours a

day, 7 days a week, 365 days a year. They not only have access to the data-
base, they have access to the professor. We joke that our students don't
really wake up until two in the afternoon and don't get onto their computers
until the evening. But they can write an expository piece and send it to the
professor anytime, any place, anywhere.

Dr. Cormier calls this "the democratization of information," and says, "I can't tell you the exhilaration I feel as a leader to know that everybody and anybody can reach me. I think it's remarkable, absolutely remarkable, when you think of how far we've come in communicating—from Morse code to this."

In San Diego, a chief deputy district attorney, Mark Whitmore, was a few years ago hired away from the DA's office in Kern County, California, to run an operation facing a difficult problem. A newly elected district attorney had discovered that the $40 million that San Diego County was collecting and paying out annually in court-ordered child support was only a drop in the bucket. Thousands of single parents were struggling to survive without the money they were supposed to be receiving from what is termed "the noncustodial parent," and the county was receiving what Whitmore calls "a tremendous level of complaint."

Mark Whitmore:

San Diego had no automated tracking to manage the cases. A consortium of
three major companies was working with California to deliver a statewide
child support system. It was due in '95, set back to '97, then declared a total
failure. It was one of the largest application failures in California's history.

Mark recalls what he found when he arrived—

We were sitting here with 185,000 cases, and other than the data processing
for the accounting that kept track of money coming through, there was

absolutely zero technology. We started developing tool sets to automate the litigation tracking, and then to automate wage assignments and so forth. And we had an incredibly powerful result. The first year we developed the automation, we processed as many cases as in the previous ten years of manual processing.

As a result, their collections went from $40 million to just shy of $120 million. There are now fifty thousand or sixty thousand children receiving support who were not receiving it previously, *"so many that you could take all those children and they would fill Qualcom Stadium. The technology made all the difference in the world."*

Initially Mark had a small team at work.

But as we went beyond, we had to bring in other people. You need to make sure you have that connection between technical people and the users. And you need to make sure you have that bridge to management. Those two are key.

And if you don't have experience managing a project like this—start small. We had really limited resources, so we picked off small pieces. We designed, developed, adjusted, implemented an individual piece, worked it through so it was successfully running. And then we'd build the next piece, and the next.

The standard procedure had always been the same as in other communities across the United States: Send out a marshal or other process server to go to the person's home, knock on the door, and hand him the summons.

We said, Why don't we first send a letter out to the house and see what happens? We found that about half the time, the people responded and came into our office. Not only did this save on the cost of service, but people showed up in a more positive frame of mind. When you send someone out to their house with a gun and badge, they're less likely to participate willingly.

Whereas technology had been in accounting systems for a long time, as it had been in engineering and inventory control, only recently has it begun to be applied in the area of social service. In San Diego, the result has been phenomenal—we have seen an increase in operational efficiency and a corresponding increase in our ability to provide quality public service.

Freightliner, a company we wrote about in an early chapter, is the number one manufacturer of heavy trucks and the largest commercial vehicle manufacturer in North America, turning out nearly 200,000 vehicles a year. More than fifty years old, the firm is now a wholly owned subsidiary of DaimlerChrysler. Freightliner as a brand is about twice the size of any of its closest competitors, and that success is in no small measure due to a commitment by a CEO who has kept the company on the bleeding edge of technology.

Jim Hebe:

In my way of thinking today, technology is the principal differentiation in your business—in your products, in your customer support, in your sales, marketing, engineering, and manufacturing.

It's the principal way we can improve the quality of our products, provide for more efficient operations of our businesses, achieve faster times to market with new products, and provide a higher level of customer support.

Jim offered three examples of how Freightliner has been gaining a competitive advantage by the aggressive, innovative use of technology—each more impressive than the next.

The first example shows how the company dealt with a complication brought on by technology itself.

Jim Hebe:

Our trucks are so complex electronically today that we say we've got more computing power in our dash than NASA had when they launched the first space shuttle—as many as seventeen computers on a single truck: collision warning systems, lane-guidance systems that alert the driver when he's going outside of his lane of traffic, electronic braking, automatic shift.

But how do you service vehicles that are so complex? And when something goes wrong with a vehicle in the field, how can a technician be equipped to diagnose the problem and repair it?

We were able to develop a system called ServicePro that uses artificial logic. Built into the memory bank of the service computer is a database that includes similar situations and the corrective actions that fixed the problem in the past.

So now when a truck goes in to a repair shop, the computer runs an analysis and then in effect says, Okay, here's what I think is the problem, here's the time it will take to fix it.

Beyond that, ServicePro is tied in to other systems, to alert the service writer, This repair is not covered under warranty but the owner has an approved credit line, and the parts are in stock.

This is the most sophisticated truck diagnostic system ever developed in this industry anywhere in the world.

Which must be a great competitive sales feature.

When a business places technology at the core of its thinking, powerful ideas can percolate up from below—as demonstrated in Jim's next example.

Our niche traditionally has been as a manufacturer with the highest customization rate of any company in the business. But in 1995, the manufacturing group came to me and said, "We think if we don't do something significantly different in our manufacturing environment, we're not going to be able to continue building the number of products that you're asking us to build. We're going to need some technology to help us."

What they had in mind developed into something we call IMIS, Integrated Manufacturing Information System—putting a PC at every build station in our plant. The traditional manner, and what most of our competitors in fact still use, is a typical bill-of-material system, where all the assembler has is a handful of paper with part numbers on it.

For each specific vehicle as it reaches a particular assembly station, we now communicate the engineering drawings, the installation drawings, the shop practices, and the installation procedures to the assembler's computer. And if that truck calls for a part like an air dryer that the worker has never seen before, the system will alert the assembly supervisor that there's something new coming.

Jim Hebe's third example, perhaps the most remarkable of all, provides the background to putting those PCs at the assembler's workstations.

This one really was an eye-opener. We put 1,200 computers in two plants and every assembly line worker who had been there from six months to thirty years became computer literate within three weeks. We went from a highly bureaucratic, paper-bound company to a totally paperless manufacturing environment in one year throughout our whole organization.

Then we took the whole system to Mexico and put it in a plant with people who couldn't even speak English—and it was an English-based system!

We just used pictures and numbers. They didn't have a clue what the description was for that part, but they knew what the number was and they knew what it looked like. Had we still been using a paper-bound system, it never would have happened. But the results are unbelievable. It's one of our best, highest quality, most efficient plants.

What accounts for their success in using technology?

Freightliner is a company that has always had a culture of wanting to be out on the edge.

But Hebe also subscribes to the view that this attitude can only start at one place.

The culture of any company of course has to be built around its leader. And if you have a culture you're trying to change or a direction you're trying to go

[in], the leader has to be more aggressive in that direction than maybe he
even believes. But you need to drag the company in that direction and you
have to do it from the top.

More than just talking the talk, the leader must provide support
for technology.

If the people in the whole organization don' t believe that the leader believes
in technology, that the leader is going to support their use of technology and
support the investment, they're not going to do it on their own—they can't
do it on their own because they need the resources, the backing, the encour-
agement, and the support to do it.

I have really encouraged our people to invest in technology, use the
power of whatever resources there were, use the power of whatever partner-
ships we have. But always to look first at what we can do to improve our own
processes, improve our systems, and use the latest in technology.

And they've known that if they had an idea that involves utilization of
technology and will improve our company or differentiate it to make our cus-
tomers more successful, they know I'm going to have an open mind to listen
to it.

You have to create an environment that says, We are a company that is
going to invest in technology, and is going to use it for continuing to maxi-
mize our competitive advantage.

All this from someone who describes himself when he became
CEO as "a person who was a technological novice."

Being on the bleeding edge of technology means leading instead of
following, taking risks instead of playing it safe, finding the newest
technology and applying it to your own business needs before your
competitors do. It means laying a path to the future . . . in more
than one sense. That was effectively summed up for us by two peo-

ple: Frieghtliner's Jim Hebe, and Don Upson, the secretary of technology for the state of Virginia.

Jim Hebe:

> I think at the end of the day when this all sorts itself out, the real winners are
> going to be those traditional producers of products or services who learn
> how to use technology. And if you don't, you're not going to be a longtime
> producer of value.

Don Upson:

> The person who builds technology systems that are responsive to the busi-
> ness side has to understand the business better than anybody. We believe
> the technology leader today in many corporations is the next generation
> chief executive officer. Because today, the technology infrastructure is the
> enterprise.

CHAPTER 14

*The Internet is a place where America has an
enormous advantage; we don't just have a
head start, we have almost the only start.
America has developed this, has understood its
capacities—because we have a free market
economy based upon entrepreneurship.*

—JIM GILMORE, **Governor of Virginia**

Using Technology as a Strategic Weapon

In the end, everything in these pages—the whole question of technology in the Digital Age—boils down to a single concept: using technology as a strategic weapon.

I've repeatedly stressed that technology must be a major focus at the highest level of the organization. And that an organization's technology group, and the leader of that group, can no longer be focused just on the plumbing, but must be able to see technology as a tool for helping to achieve the strategic goals of the organization.

You've met in these chapters a number of people who have a good command of these principles, people who have put them effectively to work in their own organizations. I end by offering a pair of men we see as exemplifying a grasp of these goals in the highest. The choice will be surprising. They are not corporate men, nor from the nonprofit world, nor from the campus . . . but from public life: Jim Gilmore, the governor of Virginia, and his chief of technology, Don Upson.

.   .   .

In 1997, when Virginia's attorney general was campaigning to become the state's governor, one plank of his program promised to make technology a focus of his administration in ways that would bring multiple benefits to the citizens and businesses of the state. It's doubtful whether many people who heard his campaign speeches recognized how unusual it was for someone with an entirely non-technical background (bachelor's degree and law degree from the University of Virginia) to be making technology a cornerstone of his platform. Nor did they understand how powerful his promises about technology would turn out to be.

The conversation about those subjects and more with coauthor Bill Simon took place in a remarkable setting—a room no larger than a big closet that is nonetheless one of the most unique offices in the country.

Governor Jim Gilmore:

> *This is the original governor's office of Virginia, the same office Thomas Jefferson sat in when he was governor. He chose to have a small office because he wanted to keep himself humble.*

The paintings Jim Gilmore has selected for the office hold a clue to his attitudes about technology.

> *I have selected as my decor portraits of four colonial leaders—Patrick Henry, James Madison, Thomas Jefferson, and John Marshall, all great Virginians. And my reason was that they were starting something entirely fresh and new, they were writing on a totally clean slate. There was nothing to guide them except their own good sense.*
>
> *I want to remember—it's my touchstone here—that those were revolutionary times and out of that revolution, a great deal of good came.*

In recruiting his team after being elected, Jim Gilmore faced the challenge of finding people who could be effective in using technology in revolutionary ways. What position would the state's technology leader hold?

> *A chief information officer would become basically an adviser to the governor and would work with the cabinet secretaries. But I rejected that model because this would be an inferior position and therefore he would be taking directional orders from the cabinet officers. I didn' t want that.*
>
> *I wanted someone who would be on an equal basis with every other cabinet official. And therefore, the only logical position was to place him on a par. He would be a cabinet-level officer, with the title secretary of technology.*

No state in the United States had a cabinet member for technology; the federal government didn't, and still doesn't. Virginia was about to become the first.

As his candidate for the post, Governor Gilmore recruited a somewhat reluctant Don Upson, who had been working at the juncture of politics and technology in Washington, D.C., and on Capitol Hill for a dozen years. There were times when Upson questioned his judgment in letting himself be talked into the job.

Secretary Upson:

> *When Governor Gilmore got elected, he called one day and said, "I'm going to make technology a cabinet post, and it'll have the control of the infrastructure for the entire state government." But I understood that no chief executive really cares how fast the computers are and how broad the bandwidth is; the governor had something broader in mind. I recommended someone for the job and he said, "Actually, I was hoping you would take it."*
>
> *A chief of technology has to have the authority, not just be the rah-rah cheerleader sitting around making statements like, "I think we should have standards." He has to have authority over the agencies to make things happen. Nobody will ever listen to him unless he has a policy responsibility.*

The functions that Governor Gilmore and Don Upson envisioned fit the prescription earlier in these pages for including an organization's technology leader at the highest executive committee of the enterprise, in a position to have an impact on strategy.

Governor Gilmore:

The secretary of technology was placed where he is for the purpose of spark-ing creativity, thinking about how you can advance things, and what kinds of goals were to be achieved. There were no previous models anywhere; no other state had ever done this, we were making this up new. So I wanted somebody who would be creative in terms of the program that would then effectuate the policy goals I had set out.

Secretary Upson:

We talked about focusing on two things: create the best business envi-ronment in the country for technology companies. And make sure all the citizens of the state are being served by the opportunities of this new economy.

Governor Gilmore:

He was to examine how we could advance the state as an environment for technology businesses, how we could make Virginia the most appealing place in America where people would want to do start-ups, where they could completely utilize their own innovation and be more creative themselves. For a state government to do this was entirely new and innovative.

The eye-opener came when Don Upson went to his first cabinet meeting.

Don Upson:

They have these executive chairs, one for the governor and one for each cab-inet officer. At the far end of the table was one little yellow chair. That one was for me. And it was stuck in at a corner—the state cabinet table did not have room for a secretary of technology.

I could almost hear them thinking, "He's not a real cabinet officer."

Oh, by the way, three months later there was a new, larger cabinet table with a real place for the secretary of technology, and a proper chair for me. So it was clear to everybody that I had the governor's support, right down to the symbolic things.

Don Upson had the governor's support on more important matters, as well, recalling that "he kept pulling me aside and saying, 'Don, is everything going okay?' He kept reassuring me, 'You're naturally going to step on toes. I just want to be sure that when you step on those toes, I'm able to come in and make sure that you're not being stopped.' "

Creating a new position that takes some traditional authority away from others clearly requires this kind of continual support.

Secretary Upson:

For this to work, we would have to put rules down for the government agencies, not just about architecture, but about standards. Now, are they all going to follow happily? No—they don't like being told what to do.

Part of Don's challenge would mean carrying out an executive order from the governor that the technology operations of every state agency were to be brought under the new Department of Technology.

The critical thing was to create buy-in, to make it a stakeholder-driven process. The governor created a Council of Technology Services, which is my internal "board of directors," to get everyone moving in the same direction.

The need for the change was compelling.

It should not take twenty-three months to negotiate a software contract, but it did when every department head had a voice, and when the bureaucratic view is to be afraid that the software company will make a profit. I now have control of that—I can make a decision and move on it.

Don had watched this struggle for years—first as a committee staff member on Capitol Hill in Washington, later working on the political side of a company negotiating technology contracts from the federal government. He found the same issues at play at the state level.

> The question is what government can do and what it should do with technology. The arguments are almost always about the traditional methods and processes, it's rarely about the technology. It's, We're the tax department, we're going to collect taxes our way, and if we do it online, we can't be online with the DMV because we don't do things the way they do their registration and drivers licenses.
>
> But the whole point is the entire enterprise has to change. We fought that with the federal government for ten or twelve years before I left, and I fought it all over again when I got here.

Don Upson's experience demonstrates once again that when the top man stands behind you with resolve, people *will* listen.

What he and the governor set out to do in Virginia, Secretary Upson says, "is not about having new computers and fast phones. It's about service." An initial goal was to make it far easier for citizens to transact business with the state government. Only two years after the Department of Technology came into being, the extent of their success can't help but impress.

> Any Virginia citizen who has an e-mail address can now be contacted via the Internet and told, "Your driver's license expires in two months, here's a PIN number; if you have a clean driving record and a credit card, you can renew online." And we're the only state where you can do this right now.
>
> Even if you let this go until the day before your license expires, you log on, in less than a minute your information is confirmed. Print out the receipt. Automatically the state police are notified and you have a paper receipt that is a valid driver's license until your real license shows up in the mail.

*Once you have a PIN number from a transaction with one state agency,
you never have to enter all your information again. You can go online at a single Web site to pay your taxes, register your cars, renew your driver's
license, make reservations at a campground, even enroll your kids in a state
college. Now that's government service the way it should work.*

Virginia has for some time had excellent technical-training programs, statewide, at both the high school and college levels. But
graduates found that technology companies in the state only wanted
to hire people with some experience; with a desperate shortage of
technical people in Silicon Valley, Redmond, Austin, and elsewhere,
many of these young people were leaving Virginia, never to return.
The state was training a valuable labor pool, then losing its talents.

Governor Gilmore and Don Upson created an internship program, under which Virginia's technology companies hire five thousand students every year. In a student's first year of part-time
interning, the company receives a tax incentive to offset the cost. If
the student returns to the same company for a second year, half the
benefit goes to the company, half toward helping to defray the student's tuition costs. The third year, all of the benefit goes toward the
student's tuition.

Result: graduates who can point to enough experience to land a
job with a Virginia technology company.

Clever, innovative, and benefiting the students, the companies,
and the technology base of the state. It's the kind of standout thinking about the use of technology as a strategic weapon that makes me
believe the Gilmore-Upson team offers such a good example for
corporate managers.

Reaching out even more directly to the people, Virginia has
launched an initiative "to bridge the 'Digital Divide' between technology haves and have-nots."

Seventy percent of U.S. teenagers say they would give up television before giving up their computers or the Internet; an even greater number say it's now "in" to be online—on a par with dating and partying! Yet the hard truth is that not all teens—or their parents—are lucky enough to have an e-mail address, much less access to a computer.

So Virginia's new "Infopowering" program aims to bring technology to those citizens who have been until now left out. Funded by a consortium of the state, private businesses, and more than a dozen nonprofit organizations, the program will place computers and high-speed Internet access at every local library in the state. A classroom program, meanwhile, will seek to identify teachers who have developed the most effective methods for using technology to enhance education, and then train other teachers to use these methods.

What's the lesson in this for the enterprise? Easy: Your "citizens" are your customers, your employees, your suppliers, and your investors. Once you have established a proper role for technology within your own company, you will then face the greater challenge of bridging the Digital Divide for your stakeholders by helping them, as well, to become part of the technology solution instead of remaining part of the technology problem.

On another front, the governor and his technology secretary recognized that the technology companies of Virginia represented a powerful source of ideas and energy for solving state problems. After all, as Jim Gilmore points out, "more than half of all the Internet traffic in the world runs through Virginia." But how do you get many companies with diverse interests working together?

The answer came in the form of a Governor's Commission on Information Technology, and the list of Virginia technology folks who have accepted an active membership role is truly impressive—a good example of the support it's possible to gather around important technology issues. The roles of the commission include people of the caliber of Steve Case, CEO of AOL/Netscape; Mike Daniels, Chairman of Network Solutions; and senior executives of the Virginia-based operations for companies like Gateway, MCI-World-Com, and Motorola. I was asked to be keynote speaker at the commission's first meeting, which led to the governor asking me to serve on the committee, representing Microsoft; I accepted and have been serving gladly, and admiring their work.

The commission has been very successful in helping establish a climate that has drawn many new technology companies to Virginia, and even in getting companies to put facilities in remote parts of the state where there is a talent pool of technically skilled people but not enough jobs.

Governor Gilmore:

We're now a marketing agent for Virginia companies, and that's a different model for government.

And the message to other corporations is, If you come to Virginia, you will have a partnership with government that's unlike any other place in the world, in terms of taxes, regulatory, marketing opportunities, networking opportunities. We show them we can have a positive effect on their bottom line.

The message of the Virginia success story, again, is recognizing that technology isn't just hardware and software and network routers anymore; it must be a cornerstone of how you do business.

Secretary Upson:

I met a senior buyer for a major retailer, and I said, "Are you moving your products online?" She said, "No, we'll be so slow in doing that, we're a $35 billion company." And all I thought was, That's too bad, there goes that company. Because Main Street has to intersect with "e-street." Old world does have to meet new world in everything.

I don't usually like sports analogies to illustrate business points. But I found Don's analogy irresistible.

> It's about putting the technology professional in the center of the decision-making process for every function of the organization. And if you don't empower that person, you'll never be able to create the needed change within the organization—because change today is all about technology. It's about changing a football world to a soccer world.
>
> Football is a game where the coach calls the play and tells the quarter-back, who tells the team; they execute the play, and the process starts all over. That's top-down management, which—no news here—doesn't work anymore.
>
> Soccer is a game where the coach sets the environment, then mostly just sits and watches. The players have to be in constant communication with each other. The game that businesses are now playing is a soccer game, across the board.
>
> Look at the new-economy companies, the really good ones. They understand it's a soccer game.

Still, the "coach" in charge of technology is vital. What are the criteria for the job?

Governor Gilmore:

> You have to have someone who is not only totally familiar with the technology, but someone who is a people person, who can work and interact in terms of policy making. Someone who tells me how to hook up a wire is of no value to me. You need someone who can interact with people who hook up wires and yet can also run a major business. And most of all, someone who can win.

Secretary Upson:

> The governor believes, and I share his belief, that in the information economy, you can't tell people what to do.
>
> If you think about it, the concept of putting control in the hands of the

people goes back in our history as a country and our history in particular as
a state — it's what the founding fathers built this country on. It's what made
America different — that the individual has dignity.

    That was a new concept 225 years ago. Since then we have ceded a lot of
that control to the federal government.

    What information technology does, more than anything else, is it pushes
power to the individual, gives people choice, gives people control.

Two other states have now appointed cabinet-level technology secretaries, and others, including California, are moving toward doing
the same. Virginia's success in technology is also being noticed elsewhere.

Governor Gilmore:

    Technology isn't yet a cohesive operation in the federal government but
they're beginning to model after us. George Bush [at the time the Republican
presidential front-runner] is talking about creating a technology post along
the lines that we have here in Virginia.

    President Mubarak of Egypt, on a state visit to the U.S., chose to come to
Virginia because the Egyptians believe they can emulate what we're doing,
especially the way we're working with businesses. And the president of Ire-
land has now arranged to visit, as well.

What's happened in Virginia happened so fast. Two years ago most
of the United States thought of the state in terms of horse farms and
tobacco fields. Today Virginia is being recognized as a world leader
in technology.

Secretary Upson:

    I think one of the advantages we had was that it never crossed our minds we
weren't going to succeed. The attitude was, We're going to create this new

way of using technology in government. That was scary because it quickly dawned on us, My God, there aren' t the resources to do this.

We managed to do it, anyway.

Governor Gilmore:

Our focus is on working with men and women, families and children, to enhance their capacity for utilizing technology to advance the quality of their lives. What we' re doing is based on a desire to make people freer using technology as a major enabling tool, to empower and liberate individuals.

There's no story I know more vivid for depicting what can happen when an organization dedicates itself to using technology as a strategic weapon than the example of the state of Virginia.

The story offers both a challenge, and a moral. The challenge: to accept the premise of adopting technology as a strategic weapon, and placing it among the other essential tools at the very center of decision making and goal setting for the organization.

The moral: that even an organization as bureaucratic and difficult to move as a state government can yield, can be reshaped to the demands of the Digital Age by people with enough foresight and dedication.

For the continued strength of the United States—and of your own enterprise—it's essential that the commitment to technology of forward-thinking organizations like those profiled in these pages become a model and a pattern. Starting yesterday.

Good luck on the journey.

From Bill Simon

If this book is, as I ardently hope, fun to read as well as valuable, that will be because I have managed to capture the personality and spirit of Bob McDowell. Few corporate executives in my experience have as much zest for life, as much enjoyment in their work. Bob—you've made the experience a pleasure—for which, many thanks.

Without the hard-won approval of my beloved Arynne, I would never turn any manuscript over to a publisher. She is brave enough to find fault with my writing—one of the many strengths she has of which I am so very proud. But when her observations make sense, I punish her in my own inimitable way by intellectually justifying every idea, word choice, and comma. She has finally learned to make the comments and gracefully walk away. (I've recently discovered a new way to frustrate her, but that won't show up until I begin my next book.)

As consultant, friend, or relative, my wife is fiercely loyal, a quality that has become familiar to executives of Silicon Valley through her work since 1983 as a consultant, coach, and mentor to high-profile leaders of high tech. Although a wonderfully insightful writer herself, she prefers working face-to-face with people and rarely writes except under duress. Still, many who have benefited from her guidance and advice return often for a refresher of her keen wisdom at her Web site, arynne.com.

I'm more than usually indebted to Arynne this time around: Through her connections with FreeSamples.com (it's one of the companies she serves as a board member), I came to see the company founder as a practitioner of one of the business processes we wanted to explore in the book; his experiences are detailed in chapter 8.

As I write this, our darling daughter Victoria, a doctoral candidate in forensic psychology, is taking a break in the rain forest of Borneo, where she is working with baby orangutans at Camp Leakey—but will thankfully be home in time to celebrate the publication of this book. Our son Sheldon, whose group the Blues Alliance plays the Nashville nightclub scene, his wife, Merrilee, and our new twin grandchildren all share my appreciation for helping make my life full of a proud parent's pleasure.

My involvement in this project initially came about thanks to two people: Ann Hamilton of Microsoft Press, and my friend and agent extraordinaire, Bill Gladstone, head of Waterside Productions. To both, my special gratitude.

And—this is getting to be a habit—my appreciation to the best publisher/editor in the business, the incomparable Adrian Zackheim, as well as to editor David Conti.

It takes a group of support people to let a writer focus on his writing. So, special appreciation to Josie Rodriguez, our housekeeper of twenty-five years, and to Jessica Dudgeon, our admin who plans the travel, keeps the books, pays the bills, and generally keeps things on an even keel for both of us. And to Marianne Stuber, who speedily typed more than six hundred pages of interview transcripts and survived to tell the tale.

To all of you, my heartfelt thanks.

From Bob McDowell

One of the earliest lessons I learned in business was that many of your most valuable lessons come from listening to your customers. That is really the heart of this book—Microsoft customers sharing with me things they have learned. Without their support and encouragement, and their enthusiasm to be part of this project, this book would not have happened. We're extremely grateful for their help.

I have in addition been privileged to learn from hundreds of Microsoft customers I have worked with around the world over the last eleven years. That experience has been invaluable to me in doing this project.

Though I have shared many of the ideas in these pages with audiences as a public speaker in many settings, the book would not have captured those thoughts without the help of my coauthor, Bill Simon. His skill in shaping my ideas into a book that will, I think, be both enjoyable and valuable for the reader was critical in getting this done, and for that I will be forever grateful.

I have received strong encouragement and support from many people throughout Microsoft and would like to call out several for special mention. First, my boss Jeff Raikes, who not only contributed ideas expressed in the book but even insisted the completion of the book be included as a goal in my annual performance review! Steve Ballmer was one of the first people I met at Microsoft and his passion for the company is an inspiration to me and all of us who work here.

If the "crown jewels" of Microsoft reside in the intellectual capacity of the people who build our products, then the company's heart beats in the field organization made up of the people dealing with our customers every day. I've spent most of my time here working with the field organization made up of salespeople, systems engineers, consultants, and others, and they have been critical in inspiring me to complete this book. Finally, there are two other people at Microsoft who have been very important to my completing this project. First is Dianna West, my former executive assistant, who has been prodding me for years to get this done and was very helpful to me in the early stages of the effort. The second is Teri Jensen, my executive assistant for the last three years, who has been of immeasurable assistance both to Bill and me in accomplishing many of the administrative tasks to get the book done.

We are who we are in large part because of how we began our lives. My parents, Larry and Dorothy McDowell, have been models for me on how to live my life and constantly encouraged me to strive to be the best I can be. While my father did not live to see me finish the book, I hope he would have been as proud of the results as I know my mother is.

The balance in my life, along with the utmost loyalty and love that I can depend on absolutely, along with encouragement in whatever I do, comes from Lissa, my wife of thirty-two years. Sharing my life with her makes all this worthwhile in the end.

In Appreciation to the People Whose Words Appear in These Pages

The authors want to extend their great appreciation to the executives and leaders who took the time to share their views and experiences with us for this book:

Lawrence Baxter, Executive Vice President, Wachovia Bank

Guy Cavallo, CIO, City of Charlotte

Dr. Patricia P. Cormier, President, Longwood College

Janet Dang, Brio Technologies

Dennis Eck, Coles Myer

Governor Jim Gilmore, State of Virginia

Rob Hassell, CIO, Freightliner

Jim Hebe, CEO, Freightliner

Bob Herbold, COO, Microsoft

Lieutenant General Warren D. Johnson, USAF (Ret.)

David Jones, Group Chief Information Officer, Scottish Power

Archie Kane, Lloyds TSB plc (Lloyds Bank)

Helen King, Highland Inn of San Juan Island (Washington)

Steve Long, co-CIO, Credit Suisse First Boston

Jeff Malkin, FreeSamples.com

Mayor Pat McCrory, Charlotte, North Carolina

Ed McDonald, Chief Architect, Texaco

Tony Pizi, First Vice President, Merrill Lynch

Mike Pusateri, Proxicom; formerly with Marriott International

Jeff Raikes, Group Vice President, Sales, Marketing and Service, Microsoft

Major General Anthony Raper, Chief Executive, Defence Communication Services Agency, U.K.

Colin Sharman, Chairman, KPMG International

Mike Turillo, Global Knowledge Officer, KPMG International

Don Upson, Secretary of Technology, State of Virginia

Mark Whitmore, Chief Deputy District Attorney, San Diego County